EMPATHETIC

HOW TO BUILD TRUST AND DRIVE RESULTS

LEADERSHIP

ISBN: 979-8-9892734-1-6
LCCN: 2023923389

This publication is designed to provide accurate and authoritative information with regard to the subject matter covered. It is sold with the understanding that the publisher is not engaged in rendering legal, accounting, or other professional advice. If legal advice or other expert assistance is required, the services of a competent professional should be sought. The opinions expressed by the authors in this book are not endorsed by SuccessBooks® and are the sole responsibility of the author rendering the opinion.

Most SuccessBooks® titles are available at special quantity discounts for bulk purchases for sales promotions, premiums, fundraising, and educational use. Special versions or book excerpts can also be created to fit specific needs.

For more information, please write:

SuccessBooks®
3415 W. Lake Mary Blvd. #950370
Lake Mary, FL 32746
or call 1.877.261.4930

EMPATHETIC

HOW TO BUILD TRUST AND DRIVE RESULTS

LEADERSHIP

SuccessBooks®
Lake Mary, Florida

CONTENTS

CHAPTER 1

EMPATHETIC LEADERSHIP: THE TWO-WORD TEST

BY CHRIS VOSS

Here's the scene. You're in talks with a terrorist...or a colleague...or an unhappy client (sometimes they all seem to run together). The point is you're in a conversation where you're practicing Tactical Empathy.

Your late-night FM DJ voice is low, paced, and calming. You're moving the conversation with focused 'what' and 'how' questions: *"What stands in the way?" "How much trouble would X get you in?"* You mirror your counterpart's words and label their feelings: *"You seem anxious about this section." "It looks like that bothers you."*

Tactical Empathy is hardly a fixed script. You may backtrack some. You may jump ahead. But by degrees the insights come and the fog lifts...

And then you do it. You take a breath and recap not your position but theirs. You paraphrase their feelings, their motivations—the energy in their stance. You say it as well or better than they would.

And you wait...and wait. The Black Swan Group teaches 'dynamic silence.' And then, instead of a stare, an 'um-hum,' or one more robotic 'yes', somewhere inside your counterpart a wall tumbles and you hear, "That's right." Not, "You're right," but the platinum "That's right."

"That's right," she's saying. "What you just put into words is the total and complete truth." Inside her, by the way, her brain is releasing a crazy one-way bonding neurochemical called oxytocin, producing a light euphoria. She's in. You can see collaboration from here because she feels understood. A new outlook and new behaviors are possible.

TACTICAL EMPATHY, a.k.a. TRUST-BUILDING

People have interesting reactions to seeing 'Empathy' and 'Tactical' together. *Empathy*, they think, *Isn't that negotiation suicide?* And *'Tactical'?...That sounds like manipulation.*

No, and no. The Black Swan Method pairs tactical and empathy to express a neutral the way a scalpel is a neutral. In a surgeon's hands it can give life; in the wrong hands it can kill. So do we lock up all the scalpels?

As a hostage negotiator, I felt no sympathy for Al Qaeda. At the same time I wanted them to bond with *me* so I could influence their behavior. I even went so far as to reframe my thinking with the mindset that "The adversary is the situation."

Tactical Empathy, as a mechanism to show understanding and to create bonding, is a mercenary tool as well as a missionary tool – its uses are subject to the user. Use it to manipulate, and relationships will eventually be doomed. Word will get out that you can't be trusted. Use the same powers for good, and you'll find yourself surrounded by phenomenal people.

Empathy began as an interpretation of a German term: *Einfühlung* (pronounced eín-fhoo-loong), which means 'in-feeling' or 'feeling into'. It was about 'feeling' art; fully grasping what the artist was expressing.

In the middle of the last century Carl Rogers was a pillar of thought in psychotherapy. He'd say empathy is entering the perspective of the other person without fear or judgment. The goal is to achieve understanding on a deep level. The foundation of that understanding comes only from reflective listening—the kind I learned before the internet, before cell phones, when I was working on a crisis hotline.

There are two aspects to the term 'reflective' here. The first is that you are reflecting back their words and meaning here so they can hear it back, and you become a great sounding board.

The second, and equally important, is that you reflect upon it. You think about it and attempt to supply insights to that person they may have become blind to regarding the motivations behind their own behavior and choices.

Another thought leader in the field is Bob Mnookin, former Chair of the Program on Negotiation at Harvard Law School and author of *Beyond Winning*. His chapter two ("The Tension Between Empathy and Assertiveness") is still the best chapter on empathy I've ever read. Every person who becomes a Black Swan coach is instructed to read this chapter and 'absorb it into your DNA.' Mnookin says empathy is not agreement. It's not even liking the other side.

When you draw this fine line on what empathy is, and isn't, it becomes a limitless skill. *Limitless*. It requires no common ground nor agreement. It's information gleaned from inside the other person.

A very interesting perspective for what closely resembles Tactical Empathy comes from Daniel Goleman, a journalist, psychologist and author of the seminal book *Emotional Intelligence*. Another of his books, *Focus: The Hidden Driver of Excellence* has a chapter entitled 'The Empathy Triad'. Goleman's definition of the three types of empathy are: cognitive, emotional and empathic concern. The way he describes cognitive empathy is very close to the way The Black Swan Group describes Tactical Empathy. The people often best at it, Goleman says, interestingly, are…*sociopaths*.

And why does he say that? Why would sociopaths instinctively adopt this approach? Because it works…because it's durable and low maintenance. Sociopaths are not known for their work ethic. Certainly not for compassion. They merely want to influence as many people as possible, as intensely as possible, for the least amount of effort.

In business, and these are my words, Tactical Empathy is the world's great hack for influence and for results.

13

TACTICAL RESULTS

I'm in an airport in Malaysia, about to miss the flight to my next meeting in Australia. The immigration line looks to me to be at least a half hour long, and my flight boards in 20 minutes. I'd like to shift the blame onto someone else, anyone else, but I got myself in this mess.

Seeing a Malaysian government bureaucrat, I cut out of line to approach him. It's no stretch to think his last worry that day is how to cover for some spoiled American who couldn't manage to arrive in time.

"I'm so sorry. I'm running late," I say. "My flight leaves in 20 minutes, and if I can't move up in line, I'm gonna miss it."

"Why are you late?" he says. His arms are crossed. I see him take in the guy that I just jumped in front of, probably thinking I deserve to go back now to the end of the line.

"It was completely my fault," I say. "I may be the stupidest person you talk to today."

Pause. What do you suppose that guy with my outbound destiny in his hands is thinking at this moment? He's thinking: *That's right.* At this point, not only am I not blowing smoke his way, but I'm also the witness for the prosecution in the case against me. *"I did it."* It's human to resist arrogance, but candor, unvarnished honesty, is disarming. The man in the uniform reaches for my passport and tickets and stamps them both. He even says, "Have a nice flight."

What got me on the plane to Australia that day is what can get anyone through meetings, contracts, negotiations, and faceoffs on any day. Acknowledge the elephant in the room and get the 'that's right.' Frankness—truth—makes collaboration possible. You acknowledge how things look to them, what they see as weaknesses and problems. When you show respect for the side you disagree with or hope to persuade...you build trust. And trust drives results.

Let's take that to the next level.

THE ACCUSATION AUDIT

When there's an elephant in the room what do you do? Do you deny it's there? No. That makes you look stupid at best and deceitful at worst. Do you ignore it? Well…that's better than denying it, yet you still look oblivious at best. The best strategy? Call it out and you know what you get? You at least look like a straight-shooter and you may get a meeting cleared of elephants. The Accusation Audit is your labor-saving device to dismiss pachyderms, advance trust, and get to the results you want.

"I'm about to sound greedy with this number," you may say. *"You're probably thinking management is always changing midstream."…"You probably resent that we've changed the deal significantly."*

Call it preemptive candor. Whatever the term, an Accusations Audit lists every terrible thing your counterpart could say about you *before they can say it*, relieving them of the need to bring it up.

But wait, you think: "The elephant is a *negative*. I'm supposed to declare every negative? Are you crazy? Isn't this when I want to bury the elephant under a pile of positives?"

No, because the longer you ignore an elephant the bigger it gets. Acknowledge the obvious and your adversaries lose their need to shoot at it. Hijackers drop emotions. Colleagues drop their guard. It's astonishing. With every negative—every accusation—in the open, two sides create a safety zone of honesty and trust.

Does it help to know the Accusations Audit has legal precedent? In an opening statement to 'get the uglies out first,' a savvy lawyer will mention all reasons the jury will dislike, even despise, the accused, to weaken, if not make the elephants disappear entirely.

If something in you strongly initially resists the Accusations Audit, that means you're human. Your survival / fear centers are designed to kick into high gear when faced with the unknown. Fear is the mind-killer.

Don't let fear or pride deprive you of a world-changing tool. Many 'truths' are a paradox. Vulnerability is often power.

GETTING STARTED

The first section of this chapter introduces the building blocks of Tactical Empathy. The foundation is your tone of voice, which can soften a harsh statement or put starch in a soft one. The Black Swan Group urges our clients to find their soothing 'late-night FM DJ' tone of voice. Upward inflections imply a question, downward inflections show understanding. In that voice you mirror and label, affirm and defuse. Denials or disagreements are off the table. You're there to understand and influence, not to debate. The other person needs to feel heard.

You seem worried about the time you need – is a label on a feeling; or...*It looks as if you want to protect the first agreement.* You even put words to negative perceptions: *It might seem as if I'm ignoring your suggestion.*

Every person you deal with—*every single person*—regardless of the outcome, should feel respected by having interacted with you. In a hostage situation in the Philippines, three weeks after the hostage walked out free, the losing terrorist called the government negotiator. He still had the negotiator's cell number. He opened with, "Did you get promoted? You're really good at what you do. They should promote you."

This terrorist was probably a sociopath, and at the same time he was human. He felt the negotiator's respect. He responded to it. The negotiator never lost sight of the fact that he was dealing with another person. In spite of losing the negotiation, the terrorist called to say in effect, *I felt respected by you. I'd deal with you again.*

Maya Angelo said, "People don't remember what you say, they remember how you made them feel." Tactical Empathy takes less time and earns greater results than any other approach.

The Black Swan message of Tactical Empathy is that it is perishable. To have it in working order when you need it, you practice every chance you get. You never stop practicing because Tactical Empathy is a life skill.

If you've been listening, at this point you might say to me, "So Tactical Empathy was created in the field, is continually researched, science-backed, is often counterintuitive, and ultimately is the surest and most direct route to real leadership?"

That's right.

About Chris

Chris Voss is the bestselling author of *Never Split the Difference*, former lead international FBI kidnapping negotiator, and CEO and founder of The Black Swan Group.

During his 24-year career with the FBI, Chris served as the FBI's hostage negotiation representative for the National Security Council's Hostage Working Group and has represented the U.S. at two international conferences. He's been recognized for a number of awards, including the Attorney General's Award, and the FBI Agents Association Award for Distinguished and Exemplary Service. He has received negotiation training from the FBI, Scotland Yard, and Harvard Law School.

Since retiring from the FBI, Chris has earned his Master's in Public Administration from Harvard University, and taught at a number of esteemed institutions, including the University of Southern California Marshall School of Business, Georgetown University, Harvard University, Northwestern University, the IMD Business School in Lausanne, Switzerland, and the Goethe Business School in Frankfurt, Germany.

Following the success of his book *Never Split the Difference*, Chris co-authored a book with real estate guru, Steve Shull, *The Full Fee Agent*, which provides practical and skillful negotiation techniques for real estate agents—both experienced and expert. Chris has been featured on podcasts and media outlets such as *TIME Magazine*, CNN, CNBC, the Lex Fridman podcast, Inc., and others.

His company, The Black Swan Group, established in 2008, aims at providing negotiation coaching for professionals all over the world through corporate and individual coaching, as well as live events.

When he isn't coaching or giving keynote speeches, Chris is passionate about learning, working out, reading, and spending time with his family. He currently lives in Las Vegas.

To connect with Chris and his company, you can go to:

- blackswanltd.com

You can also follow him on LinkedIn and Instagram.

CHAPTER 2

WHAT I'VE LEARNED ABOUT LEADERSHIP AS A 'DISEASE DETECTIVE'

BY JENNIFER LEE
– FOUNDER AND CEO, JLC LIFE SCIENCES

Cancer, akin to a thief, robs us of loved ones. Perhaps it was the elusive nature of the disease that drew me to the sharp, analytical world of Sherlock Holmes, thereby serving as the primary source of inspiration for my life's work in cancer treatments.

My father introduced me to the stories as a child, and from those tales I was inspired to approach cancer research with the same keen observation, aiming to unravel its mysteries. Growing up in South Korea, the Arthur Conan Doyle tales my father shared with me ignited a profound curiosity within me. They instilled an intense desire to solve problems by diligently examining the evidence.

LOSS, LEARNING, AND THE QUEST FOR A CURE

Following the clues over the past twenty-plus years in the healthcare world, I have been privileged to play a part in the development of seven first-in-class therapies that are now widely used in around 140 countries—helping countless patients worldwide. More importantly, for me, these patients have experienced extended, fulfilling lives due to these therapies.

That early curiosity I developed was shaped toward helping others by two painful losses within the space of a year or so. My beloved grandfather died of cancer after years of suffering for which he could not get the treatment he needed. While I was still mourning his passing, my father was in a bad automobile accident. Because his severe internal injuries were not detected in time, he died the following day.

As a seven-year-old, I did not understand all that had happened to these two men I loved, and why, but I was determined to do whatever I could to shield others from such devastating, preventable tragedies. In my younger days, I was captivated by marine life. I envisioned myself standing in front of a classroom, enlightening eager minds about the mysteries of the ocean.

However, as the realities of life came into sharper focus, I recognized the challenges that lay ahead. The long journey to such a profession, with its financial and time commitments coupled with my family's financial situation, was a distant dream, causing me to rethink and adapt my aspirations.

THE AMERICAN DREAM AND PROFESSIONAL BREAKTHROUGHS

Upon setting foot in the United States, I decided to pursue biochemistry, which opened up a whole new world. A college internship with G.D. Searle, then a small pharmaceutical company, gave me an opportunity to collaborate with the pioneering team behind the development of *Celebrex*, a groundbreaking pain reliever used as an arthritis medication. This enriching experience led to a full-time position, granting me vital real-world experience and invaluable insights into the pharmaceutical landscape.

Such hands-on participation proved indispensable when I later chose to further my academic pursuits—earning a master's degree in Clinical Research and Regulatory Administration from Northwestern University. The combination of real-world experience and academic training equipped me uniquely for the challenges in the pharmaceutical landscape.

During my twenty-six years in the drug industry, I've been privileged to help drive some seminal drug advancements. Among them, *Orserdu*, a drug approved by the FDA, which is the first and only oral treatment for postmenopausal women and adult men with ER-positive, HER2-negative, ESR1-mutated advanced or metastatic breast cancer after progression on endocrine therapy.

LEADING WITH EMPATHY AND PRECISION

Developing groundbreaking therapies in the pharmaceutical and biotech sectors demands more than mere scientific knowledge; it calls for a unique, multidimensional blend of empathy and determination.

At the forefront is our empathy for the patients we aim to serve. While the intricate process of creating effective drugs requires patience, there's an urgency to this endeavor. This sense of pressing need should resonate with every team member involved; each passing day might deprive a patient of a life-altering remedy. Perhaps, in the extended months we are able to give someone, another innovative treatment might emerge.

Time is of the essence, as is effectiveness. That means we set ourselves high standards. We have clear goals, and we hold ourselves and each other accountable to them. We don't let things slide. If there are missed deadlines or mistakes, we face them square on and talk about how we are going to course correct and avoid repeating the error.

My guiding principle is simple – address issues decisively while treating individuals with kindness. Leadership begins at the helm, ensuring your team members understand they have your unwavering support while exemplifying relentless dedication. This commitment might manifest as being the earliest bird and the last to depart. There may need to be some straight-talking behind closed doors, but outwardly your team needs to be confident that you believe in and support them. I often use the illustration of rowing with my teams: just as in a boat, synchronized efforts prevent us from veering off course or, worse yet, capsizing.

Internal empathy to the organization means recognizing that people are more than just their skills. Someone may be struggling to deliver because they have a situation in their personal lives that is affecting them. It's important they know you understand and sympathize, but also that there is a sense of team responsibility which means they feel able to come to you to explain when things might be hard, rather than wait until their performance is negatively impacted.

Personal empowerment is vital too. When team members feel they have some freedom to initiate, they rise to the challenge. That was my experience when I was asked to step in a few years ago with a company whose promising breast cancer drug project had stalled, with no patients enrolled for the next important round of trials.

I discovered a bigger problem than I had anticipated: a small team that was lacking in direction, discouraged, and divided. I needed to be a tough parent, balancing warmth with clear expectations. Some people needed to be let go and new team members recruited who bought into the vision. It was demanding, but we rallied around our shared goal and within just fifteen months had recruited almost five hundred patients for a trial that paved the way for bringing that new drug to the market soon. At the core of that turnaround: a bold vision, shared convictions, and relentless drive.

A MOTHER'S LEGACY: STRENGTH IN ADVERSITY

Developing this rounded sense of empathy has been a process, a journey of discovery. If there's one single person who most shaped me into the woman I am today, it's my mother. I'm awed when think of the resilience she showed on being left a widow at the age of thirty-eight, with four small children to raise—at a time when South Korea was not as prosperous as it is today.

We lost everything virtually overnight. Within a short time of my father's death, the members of his board sold the company from under us. Even before the funeral, officials from the bank came round to our home and yellow-stickered everything that could be sold off—including my precious Barbie doll.

With no qualifications, my mom called friends and acquaintances to ask if there was anything she could do to earn a little money—clean their home, clean their restaurants. All this while trying to shield us from the stress, as we coped with the loss of our beloved father.

Unable to stay in our home, it looked like we would be out on the streets until a church stepped in to help. They allowed us to move into a small, one-bedroomed apartment that was part of the facility. It wasn't much for a family of five, but at least we still had a roof over our heads. We ate a lot of ramen noodles.

Throughout it all, my mother never complained. Though she was heartbroken, she lived without regrets. And even though we were barely scraping by, she was always aware of the needs of others and continued to encourage us to be generous and thoughtful—even when it hurt.

One bright point following my father's death was that, somehow, we had been able to hold onto a beautiful grand piano we owned. Not only was it a connection to happier times, but it was also a source of comfort for my sister and me, as we taught ourselves to play. Then, one day when I came home from school, the piano was gone. Mom had donated it to a church, saying their need was greater than ours. I cried, but in time I would come to see her selflessness in what she did and appreciate her all the more for it.

Mom's quiet strength saw us through the turbulence of immigrating to the United States when I was a teenager. Being able to join relatives was a great opportunity, of course, but it was still challenging. Arriving without understanding a word of English, we nestled into a modest townhouse in Park Ridge, a Chicago suburb, sharing space with our aunt, uncle, and three cousins. Mom never sought any kind of public aid, working relentlessly across multiple jobs to provide for us. All this as a minority woman in a foreign country: I learned profound resilience.

Adolescence can be hard enough, without the additional challenges of a new culture and language. I was determined not to add to Mom's burdens, though, so I studied diligently to assimilate. I'd go to school, then walk several miles to a doctor's office where I worked in the office. I'd leave there at 8 p.m. or 9 p.m., get home and eat dinner before doing my homework in the early hours.

I was a dutiful student, but one day I was so tired I slept through a whole high school chemistry exam. The teacher, Mr. Guthrie, woke me at the end, his eyes filled with understanding. I recall he gave me an A for the class, but more importantly, he granted me a lesson in compassion and support.

PARTNERS IN LIFE AND LEADERSHIP

While my mother exemplified the gentle touch of genuine empathy, my partner, Daniel Song, has shown me that leadership doesn't always means wielding an iron fist. Instead, true leadership is a graceful blend of compassion and conviction, a balance between understanding and decisiveness. Since our college days, Daniel has built a highly successful dental practice while also venturing into fruitful real estate opportunities.

Throughout his journey, he has demonstrated the fine art of merging heart with hard lines—nurturing a business with care while ensuring accountability. In addition, he has always been my unwavering pillar, not only supporting my professional desires, but also helping me realize them. For example, he managed our bustling household with three young children (and two pets!) during a period when I was a weekly 'super-commuter' between Chicago and California.

PIONEERING A COLLECTIVE FUTURE IN LIFE SCIENCES

As rewarding as all the breakthroughs I have participated in have been, a deeper urge within me yearned for an even broader impact. That desire propelled me to found JLC Life Sciences. Through consultation and guidance for other entities in the life sciences field, I aim to leverage my expertise, catalyzing greater advancements in the field.

It also affords me an opportunity to engage more broadly within the industry, from delivering keynote speeches to contributing to prestigious, peer-reviewed journals and guest columns. A key challenge I'm advocating for is to see companies share some of the unsuccessful data from their trials, to expedite the research journey for others. While I recognize the need to protect competitive intelligence, a degree of collaboration could be the key to faster therapeutic innovations. Instead of the standard fifteen-year timeline for cancer drug development, why not cooperate and try to reduce that to a mere five years?

While some may dismiss this vision as mere wishful thinking, history begs to differ. The rapid development of the COVID-19 vaccine is an example of our collective capability when we unite with purpose and urgency. And let's not forget Apollo 11. In 1961, when President Kennedy set the audacious goal of landing a man on the moon within the decade, many deemed it a fantastical dream. Yet, eight years later, Neil Armstrong climbed out of Apollo's lunar module and famously declared, "One small step for man, one giant leap for mankind."

In addition to consulting, I have ventured into active investing, with a particular interest in championing women-led life sciences companies. This drive is deeply rooted in my personal experience with financial instability, knowing how it can be a barrier to personal progress. Plus, despite all the advances we have seen, women-led companies currently still receive a mere 1% of the available funding. This is even more perplexing given the evidence that women-owned businesses often outperform others, from generating higher revenue to dealing with challenges such as product recalls.

Though much of my work has centered on treating sickness, a mission undeniably crucial, I am increasingly convinced of the imperative to pivot toward prevention, an area in which some of these new life sciences companies I champion are pioneering.

ADVERSITY AS THE ULTIMATE TEACHER

I learned early that life unfolds unpredictably, and we aren't always in control. In the short time between the deaths of my grandfather and then my father, life tested us further with a devastating house fire that originated from a neighboring apartment. My family lost everything in the middle of the night. I fled in just my pajamas, jumping from the fourth floor onto an inflatable escape chute.

Along with our bereavements, this experience made me realize that sometimes all we can determine is how we choose to respond – do we let circumstances dictate our path, or do we arise, defiant and undeterred? Every challenge, rather than breaking me, honed my resilience. I emerged stronger and adaptable, with a keen sense of foresight, and an unyielding thirst for knowledge.

SEIZING THE MOMENT

While risk management is crucial, especially in the complex world of drug development, even flawless planning must recognize its own limitations. Calling again on the metaphor of rowing, I frequently emphasize to my teams the importance of reading the weather for signs of storms.

Yet, when challenges arise, it's essential to embrace determination over despair. We need to be continuous learners, surrounding ourselves with those who are ahead of us and from whom we can glean wisdom. In doing so, we can develop our intuition and are better equipped to respond thoughtfully to challenges, rather than simply react.

As Sherlock Holmes meticulously examined clues to solve mysteries, I too have scoured the scientific world for answers to one of humanity's greatest foes—cancer. My story, intertwined with love, loss, and the indomitable spirit of human resilience, serves as a beacon of hope for those seeking to transform challenges into life-changing opportunities. I believe we all need to seize every opportunity to make the most of the one life we are given—not just for ourselves, but for those we can uplift.

About Jennifer

A globally-recognized strategist, Jennifer Lee has always believed in the mantra, "Science holds the potential to change lives, and it's our duty to bridge the gap." As the founder and CEO of JLC Life Sciences, based in Chicago, Jennifer has seamlessly turned this belief into reality. Her consulting firm specializes in translating breakthrough scientific advances into life-saving treatments, earning the trust of prestigious clients across the U.S., Europe, and Asia. Jennifer's impact on the therapeutic frontier has been profound over the last two decades. The therapies she's championed have culminated in a $20 billion value, echoing her unmatched expertise and dedication. Her leadership, celebrated for its blend of honesty, integrity, and deep industry insight, consistently guides companies through the complexities of regulatory mazes and challenging projects.

But Jennifer's vision isn't limited to consulting. She's an ardent advocate for economic equality, particularly championing the cause of women of color. As an investor, she's betting on the future, directing her efforts towards promising science and technology frontrunners poised to dominate the global stage. Moreover, she's working to address the mounting concern of digital data waste.

In addition to her leadership at JLC Life Sciences, Jennifer holds multiple board and advisory positions, contributing her expertise to both private and non-profit sectors. She is a frequent face at the industry summits sharing her insights and inspiring the next generation of innovators.

Jennifer graduated from the University of Illinois at Chicago with a bachelor's degree in Biochemistry and a master's degree in Regulatory Compliance from Northwestern University. Outside the boardroom, Jennifer is deeply involved with How Women Lead, CANCER FUND, Vanderbilt University Startup, Springboard Enterprises, and Women in Bio Chicago 3.8, underscoring her commitment to fostering entrepreneurship and nurturing budding ecosystems.

You can contact Jennifer at:

- LinkedIn: Jennifer Lee | https://www.linkedin.com/in/jennifer-h-lee-/
- X (formerly twitter) Jennifer Lee (@Jennife26937267) / X (twitter.com)
- Instagram: Jennifer Lee (@jennifersong2222
- Email: jennifer@jlclifesciences.com

CHAPTER 3

HARNESSING EMPATHY

BY KARRIE BURNS

In the center of a large horse arena, a chestnut stallion stood relaxed and composed. A woman, participating in an equine leadership program, entered the arena. Eager to prove her ability to lead the solitary horse, she walked assertively toward him, ready to take charge. However, the horse, finely attuned to its surroundings, sensed her formidable energy. Instead of complying, it stood firmly in place, ears pinned back, as if preparing for a direct confrontation. In this tense moment, an unspoken power struggle unfolded as the woman, aware of the horse's imposing presence, abruptly stopped cold in her tracks. The horse's unexpected resistance triggered an unfamiliar vulnerability within her.

Shortly after, another participant ventured into the arena, eager to connect with the beautiful horse. She approached him warmly, anticipating a reciprocal display of affection. In her optimism, she assumed her amiable disposition would effortlessly lead to a positive interaction. However, once again, the horse defied expectations. It avoided eye contact, retreated, and displayed signs of unease. Overwhelmed by her longing for connection, she eventually left the arena, tears welling up, perplexed by why the horse hadn't responded to her affection. In her eagerness, she had unintentionally overlooked the horse's preferences, concentrating solely on her own desires.

Finally, a third woman entered the arena, her demeanor a stark contrast to the previous two. She approached cautiously, concerned that the horse might neither want nor allow her to get close. Moving slowly yet purposefully, she observed how the horse reacted to each step she took. She refrained from rushing or imposing her will upon the horse, patiently waiting to discern its response. To her astonishment, the horse gracefully lowered itself to the ground, putting her at ease. It was as if the horse had intuited her need, silently communicating, "I understand that you need me to be smaller so you can approach."

LESSONS IN EMPATHY

These three interactions with the same animal illustrated that horses, as highly intuitive and empathetic beings, respond differently based on an individual's nonverbal body language, energy, motives, and approach. For horses, empathy is a finely-tuned survival skill. As prey animals, they have a keen ability to read their environment, sensing any abnormality or change that could pose danger. Horses use empathy to identify a leader, whether another horse in the herd or a person whom they can trust. Building rapport with a horse starts with providing them with a sense of security. Once trust is established, a horse complies, as it wants to be led by a competent and capable leader.

Equine-assisted learning can be a powerful tool; it is a learning experience I use with my clients in leadership and development training. The interactions with horses can provide individuals with a reflection of their own energy, as demonstrated in the previous scenarios.

These interactions can evoke strong emotions, compelling participants to confront unexpected insights, which lead to introspection and provoke questions such as, "How do these experiences relate to my interactions at home and at work? When might others feel similar when I walk into a room?" This introspection often leads to a deeper understanding of their interactions with others.

Consider the first scenario, where the horse mirrored an aggressive posture in response to an authoritative demeanor. The woman, who had approached with a commanding presence, realized her staff might also perceive her as overly aggressive. The experience served as a wake-up call and forced her to contemplate her own intensity with others.

In the second case, the woman's desire for friendship and affection prevented her from understanding and offering what the horse needed at that moment.

The third scenario, where the horse sensed the woman's hesitancy and nonthreatening demeanor, revealed a subtle strength and confidence that even the woman didn't realize she possessed.

These encounters demonstrate an insightful lesson about empathy, relevant not only within the horse arena but also in the broader business world. They underscore the importance of self-awareness, which is a prerequisite for developing empathy.

COACHING EMPATHETIC LEADERSHIP

As a leadership and development coach, my role involves collaborating with leaders across various levels of an organization. Through my experience, I've come to recognize that a fundamental challenge many leaders face is establishing trust within their teams.

Trust is the foundation upon which all personal relationships and successful business outcomes are built. Without trust, teams often experience a cascade of negative consequences, including diminished productivity, performance issues, low team morale, and heightened interpersonal conflicts.

The primary focus of my work with clients addresses the interpersonal challenges at work oftentimes spawned by this lack of trust. I've observed that tackling these interpersonal hurdles yields the most significant return on investment. It's a process that unfolds gradually yet consistently. Through one-on-one coaching and experiential workshops, I provide a structured framework that empowers my clients to effectively cultivate trust and empathy.

This framework is anchored in a three-step approach:

1. Start with self-awareness.
Effective leadership begins with self-awareness. Leaders must first gain a deep understanding of themselves, including their thoughts, emotions, values, beliefs, and behaviors that influence their interactions with others.

2. Balance your warmth and competence.

People assess their leaders based on two characteristics: warmth (how likable, trustworthy, and caring they appear) and competence (how strong, capable, and influential they seem). While everyone leads with a primary characteristic, they can work to strengthen the other. Understanding and adapting your style to meet the needs of another person requires both self-awareness ("How do I naturally come across to others?") and empathy ("Should I adapt my style to effectively match the needs/preference of another?"). Practicing this skill is both enlightening and engaging.

3. Connect with empathy.

This approach emphasizes the importance of connecting with others on an emotional level initially—build rapport and trust by respecting others' feelings and needs. Engaging with empathy requires a delicate balance and refined skill set. When utilized effectively, empathy serves as a conduit to forming meaningful connections. It bridges gaps, lowers emotional barriers, and lays the foundation for trust.

Like many things in life, this framework, while simple, requires commitment and practice to become proficient and comfortable with these skills. However, when these principles are wholeheartedly embraced and consistently put into action, clients report transformative results.

PRACTICING EMPATHETIC LEADERSHIP

One day my eldest daughter, Emerson, who was a mere seven years old at the time, came home from school and shared a profound insight. She said, "Mommy, today we learned about empathy in school. What I realized is that William [her five-year-old brother] was born with empathy, but I think it's something I'm going to have to learn."

I was amazed at her ability to perceive that empathy can be natural for some, while others will need to actively develop the skill. Regardless of whether someone is innately empathetic, recognizing its significance and dedicating effort to enhance this skill is invaluable.

If you recognize the importance of empathy but, like Emerson, recognize it is not a natural strength, or struggle to incorporate it into your leadership practice, know that you're not alone. Many of us find empathy challenging. It can feel exhausting and uncomfortable.

These strategies may help you develop your empathetic leadership skills:

1. **Develop self-awareness**—understand yourself.

- Define your core values and beliefs.
- Journal regularly to gain insights into your behaviors.
- Take personality assessments to understand your style, tendencies, and behaviors.
- Seek feedback from trusted sources to gain an external perspective.

2. **Connect with empathy**—understand others.

- Get curious about understanding others' perspectives.
- Practice listening to understand versus to respond.
- Pay attention to nonverbal cues and body language.
- Find common interests and shared experiences.
- Ask open-ended questions and withhold judgment.
- Share stories and experiences to connect.

Developing self-awareness and embracing empathy will nurture authenticity, trust, and meaningful connections within your team. Each action you take to cultivate these strengthens you as a leader and improves your interactions with and impact on others.

A BUSINESS CASE FOR EMPATHY

In today's rapidly changing world, the importance of self-awareness and empathy cannot be overstated. These critical skills are often overlooked in traditional education, yet they are becoming increasingly vital as we navigate a landscape where artificial intelligence continues to advance.

Empathetic leadership equips individuals with essential emotional intelligence skills, ensuring their relevance and resilience in a changing environment. Research consistently demonstrates the benefits associated with empathetic workplaces, including reduced stress, enhanced collaboration, increased job satisfaction, talent retention, and cost savings.

Investing in the development of critical skills such as empathy is not just a choice; it's a strategic imperative. These skills are the linchpin of successful leaders in our evolving world. Recognizing this, forward-thinking organizations are committing resources to ensure their leaders are well-equipped in these areas.

As leaders ourselves, we understand the intrinsic value of honing these skills. They empower us to relate more effectively to our teams, make informed decisions, and navigate complex challenges. They serve as the foundation for building authentic connections and fostering a culture of trust within our organizations.

DEVELOPING EMPATHETIC LEADERS

During my time as the experiential learning leader at GE Crotonville, renowned as a premier corporate leadership institution, I had the privilege of creating global leadership programs for the company's top executives. This experience not only allowed me to learn from world-class leaders but also deepened my appreciation for the significance of empathetic leadership in the business world.

General Electric's dedication to leadership development extended far beyond conventional classroom settings. For select senior executives we designed experiential programs that pushed the boundaries of traditional learning.

These programs took our leaders to unique experiential settings, from the beaches of Normandy, retracing the steps of Allied soldiers during a pivotal battle, to the vibrant streets of Tel Aviv, exploring the culture of innovation in the heart of a 'start-up nation.' We also ventured to post-Arab Spring Egypt, immersing our leaders in the dynamic social and cultural shifts of a transitioning region, and Lagos, to get a firsthand perspective of how Nigeria's energy sector is powering economic growth in Africa.

These programs were truly unique in their approach. Instead of relying on theoretical case studies, they offered transformative real-world experiences. Each experience was thoughtfully designed to challenge our leaders' perspectives and ignite their sense of empathy. It involved stepping into the shoes of individuals from diverse backgrounds, viewing the world through unique lenses, and listening to their stories with open hearts.

It was during these moments, far removed from meetings and boardrooms, when leaders gained a profound understanding of the transformative power of empathy—an essential skill for tackling complex problems and resolving organizational conflicts.

Today, as the cornerstone of my consulting business, I continue to create unique and highly experiential programs that immerse leaders and their teams in settings that enable empathetic learning, all with the overarching goal of becoming more effective leaders.

A HUMBLE PATH TO EMPATHETIC LEADERSHIP

On a personal note, while I teach and coach leaders empathy skills, I readily admit that I am still a work in progress. Every day, I consciously strive to refine these skills, recognizing that they haven't always been second nature to me. It's this self-awareness that led me to this profession—a path where I continually learn about empathy and its profound impact on our lives. Though this process can be challenging at times, it has been undeniably transformative.

In fact, I was the woman who walked into that horse arena with the assertive demeanor during my equine leadership certification. While I understood the importance of empathy in theory, it took a memorable encounter with a horse to truly grasp how my own intensity influenced those around me. This pivotal moment allowed me to empathize with my sensitive and empathic son, realizing how he might feel when my strong presence overwhelms him—much like I felt when facing that fifteen-hundred-pound animal.

This revelation marked a turning point in my journey toward empathetic leadership. It taught me that empathy isn't just an intellectual concept;

it's a skill we develop through self-awareness and personal experiences. Just as the horse mirrored my energy back to me, our interactions with others often serve as mirrors of our own approach. It's during these moments of self-reflection that we can authentically grasp the significance of empathy in our personal and professional lives.

Becoming a parent marked one of the most insightful and humbling chapters of my life. It inspired an unwavering commitment to intentionality, especially in the realm of empathy. While understanding and responding to our children's needs may seem as if it should be instinctual, the whirlwind of work, school, extracurricular activities, and daily life often causes us to rush through the conversations and moments that cultivate empathy at home, much as we do in our professional lives.

If you've faced challenges in practicing empathy at work, I wholeheartedly encourage you to begin small, by practicing within your family. Consider using conversation cards in a playful way during a family meal to guide discussions, covering topics such as challenges faced, moments of joy, or goals for the upcoming week. The key is to use active listening and show genuine interest in each other's perspectives. This practice not only fosters empathy but also strengthens family bonds, helping everyone feel more connected and supported.

Your loved ones are an incredibly receptive audience, yearning for your understanding and connection just as deeply as anyone in your professional life. Investing the time and effort to develop empathy within your family may turn out to be the most valuable and rewarding commitment you ever make. The most vital action you can take as an empathetic leader is to practice empathy consistently in your daily interactions, especially at home, where it is most needed and valued.

The framework and practical application strategies serve as a guide. It starts with self-awareness, followed by the embrace of empathy, and culminates in taking empathetic action. By continually practicing and refining these steps, you can build trust within your teams, strengthen relationships, and create positive and inclusive work environments.

As we journey toward empathetic leadership in our various roles, let's heed the wisdom of a child's insight: Empathy is a skill we all can and should develop. It serves as the foundation of effective leadership, fostering trust, collaboration, and stronger interpersonal relationships by forging authentic connection.

About Karrie

Karrie Burns is a dynamic leadership and development coach known for creating world-class experiential learning programs that ignite growth, foster authentic connections, and elevate leadership excellence on a global scale.

Karrie's diverse career has taken her from the Department of Defense in Germany to campaign fundraising in Washington, DC, and then to leadership development roles at General Electric's Crotonville Management Institute. It was at GE where she began designing global leadership courses for the company's top 1% of senior executives, including programs in Europe, Israel, India, Nigeria, and South Korea. These enriching experiences allowed her to collaborate with industry giants like Boeing, Proctor and Gamble, 3M and IBM.

Karrie is recognized for her unique ability to craft memorable learning experiences that seamlessly weave in the human-centric aspects of leadership. An example of this approach was in an exhibit she created that was spotlighted by The Boston Globe in 2017, emphasizing the importance of gratitude as a foundational element in leadership.

Leveraging her vast experience, Karrie founded Fireside Consulting Group, which provides strategic consulting, coaching, immersive workshops, and offsite retreats tailored for leaders across organizational levels. Her programs prioritize emotional intelligence, team dynamics and leadership excellence. At the heart of her work are transformational experiences that leave a lasting impact.

Embodying the commitment to lifelong learning, Karrie extends her reach beyond the corporate settings. Collaborating with experts across various fields, she also curates personal wellness retreats, showcasing her belief that continuous growth profoundly enriches one's life. This holistic perspective is mirrored in the feedback she receives. As one leader shared, "Her programs don't just teach; they transform – on a deeply personal and professional level. She has been a driving force behind my success."

Karrie cherishes her life in upstate New York with her husband Kevin, their three children, Emerson, William and Caroline, and their beloved dog, Lily. She finds that they continually challenge and shape her understanding and commitment to the pursuit of empathetic leadership.

In the ever-evolving world of leadership, Karrie Burns stands out with her authentic approach, blending unique expertise with genuine care. She not only redefines leadership development but reshapes how it's perceived and practiced.

To learn more about Karrie and Fireside Consulting Group go to:

- Website: www.FiresideConsultingGroup.com
  or
- Email: info@firesidesideconsultinggroup.com

CHAPTER 4

PUTTING PEOPLE FIRST
LESSONS FROM MY PARENTS, PATAGONIA, AND ONE BAD HIRE

BY MARTY SNYDER

The 45-caliber Smith and Wesson box landed with a thud on the table in front of me, confirming the weight of its contents.

"I brought this for Dave," she said with a snarl.

I looked down at the box and tried not to show my emotions, currently going haywire. This was the first I was hearing about any tension or problems between Dave and anyone else on the team. Mustering all possible understanding, I carefully said, "I know Dave can be pretty obnoxious, but…"

"He needs his mouth washed out, and I plan to be the one to do it," she declared.

My senses whirled as she vented more of her frustrations. I let her speak. I knew she just needed someone to listen. After a long tirade, she paused.

"Have you shared your feelings with him?" I asked.

"I've told him, but he doesn't care," she continued. "That's why I brought this."

She reached for the gun box. It took everything I had not to wrestle her to the ground. My mind raced. We were in a corporate business park just outside Seattle in one of the city's more posh suburbs. We sat in a well-furnished conference room with professionals walking by the door. This sort of thing didn't happen.

Or did it, I wondered. Dozens of scenarios raced through my mind in the milliseconds it took her to reach for the box and open it. Then, as she removed the lid, I noticed something peculiar about the box's contents. There, inside the finely crafted, very real Smith and Wesson handgun box, was a bottle of mouthwash.

Like air escaping from a balloon, the tension left my body. Relief flowed through my veins. I tried to mask the giddiness and relief in my voice. With infinitely more composure, I said, "You must be feeling really upset."

With the mouthwash incident safely defused, I pivoted to the real reason I had called her into the meeting. I was letting her go. It wasn't a firing due to performance or behavior. (Although I suspect there were grounds for that.) I was letting her go because our project was coming to an end. There wasn't work for her or the rest of the team, including Dave, the mouthwash victim.

———≈———

Having employed 1,500 people in my career, I can say with heartfelt sincerity that I've cared about every one of them. Any upset employee is a concern for me. Not that I'm a model employer. Far from it. I'm human, and everyone makes mistakes. My mistakes could line the halls of the Smithsonian!

"I have dozens of Harvard MBAs," I like to say. "Meaning, of course, the cost of my mistakes, in dollars and lessons hopefully learned, adds up to dozens of Harvard MBAs."

At the time of the mouthwash incident, my company, Communication Infrastructure Corporation (CIC), developed wireless infrastructure. In those days, that meant temporary employment. We hired and fired regularly. Most people we hired never wanted to leave, though. They routinely said our company was the best they'd ever worked for.

What made us such a great company? One thing. Genuine concern and empathy for everyone on our team.

As the statistics show in dozens of *New York Times* bestselling business books, companies that create a culture of genuine empathy for employees consistently outperform those that don't. I saw evidence of this daily.

———≈———

Raised by a pastor and a schoolteacher, I was taught the power of empathy early on. Our family of seven grew up sharing our holiday meals (and often regular meals) with all kinds of guests. We welcomed everyone, from the janitor of Dad's church to intercity teenagers without regular dinner tables, much less holiday ones.

Mom and Dad's kindness toward others was the stuff of legends. After my father retired, health issues removed him from social life, and he slipped into obscurity. Still, hundreds of people from all walks of life showed up at his funeral. Mom was the same. They welcomed and entertained for no other reason than it was how they believed you should live your life. It became the model for me and my siblings.

By the time I entered the workforce, I thought of everyone as equals. Tyrannical bosses, I thought, were surely just literary devices—stories confined to the pages of *A Christmas Carol*. I couldn't imagine not treating everyone with respect for their dignity and security.

———≈———

At twenty-four, my girlfriend wanted a life change. We left our hometown and headed to Santa Barbara, California. I was a rock climber then, and soon after moving, I had to visit the place where rock climbing legend Yvon Chouinard and the Patagonia company got its start making carabiners and pitons.

When we visited, all the young men took an instant liking to my girlfriend. "Would you like to work here," one of them offered after discovering she was new to the area and needed a job. She agreed. The following year, our first daughter was born.

We brought our baby home from the hospital, but a health incident brought us back just two weeks later. The diagnosis was apnea, and California state law required a heart monitor for six months.

Patagonia offered three months of paid maternity leave. Our insurance coverage would lapse in ninety days. My wife shared the news with her manager, and I anxiously calculated the imminent medical bills. (In those days, I was a carpenter, and money was tight.)

Within that first week of the news, while I was at work, the phone rang. It was Malinda Chouinard, wife and business partner of Patagonia founder Yvon Chouinard.

"I just wanted you to know that we want you to stay at home for the next six months, and we're going to pay for your insurance. So, don't worry about anything." Malinda paused. "Taking care of that baby is the most important thing, and we want you back in good spirits."

My wife hung up in ecstatic tears.

------- ≈ -------

After leaving carpentry and general contracting, a trail of circumstances led me to found CIC. As we grew, so did the need to create an HR department. My firsthand experience with Patagonia influenced every benefit, healthcare, and policy decision we made.

Everyone has a built-in radar for personal empathy—a sixth sense for knowing when someone genuinely cares about you. Any team that experiences authentic empathy among its members works better and more effectively. It's like in the game of tug-of-war. The team that pulls together in unison dominates any opponent.

Every policy we made, from the hiring process to the salary and benefits, was chosen so people knew we had their best interests in mind. A service company's product is its people, and we made sure our people felt supported, well paid, and empowered with the freedom to be their best.

Deborah, our head of HR, was a recommendation from a mutual friend. She lived by the same set of values, and her staff acted as an on-call counseling department. Anyone needing support could call on them. Deborah had a saying: our employees are my customers.

The expense of our HR department was higher than a typical company in our industry, but the benefits far outweighed that cost.

———— ≋ ————

Situation after situation proved we were making the right decisions.

Once, when we were experiencing rapid growth and resulting cash flow challenges, a delayed customer payment left us without enough capital to make payroll. The sudden, unanticipated shortage would affect about ten well-paid individuals. Knowing most people live paycheck to paycheck, I realized our situation was serious.

With few options, Deborah and I sat down and studied a list of our employees. We identified fifteen people we felt comfortable asking to hold their paycheck for two weeks. We only needed ten, but we wanted a buffer.

I was the first to elect to hold my paycheck, and I knew I had to be the one to ask the others. I spent an entire day phoning everyone on the list. I explained the situation and told them I wouldn't be taking pay until the matter was resolved. The situation was difficult for most people, but every single person I asked to curtail their paycheck agreed. Some even called on family members to help them through the cash shortage.

———— ≋ ————

As the years passed, our work increasingly focused on microwave telecommunication systems. This allowed us to employ more permanent staff, so we didn't have to hire and fire for every job. We could hire, train, and retain our people and then move seamlessly from one job to the next.

I read once that the cost of hiring a new employee equals three to five months of payroll for that employee. With permanent staff specializing in our services, I reasoned it would actually be less costly to the company to pay them all year—whether we had work or not.

Paying each staff member a year-round salary without year-round projects was challenging. We had to honor a large payroll without the supporting revenue. But after a dry spell, it was always rewarding and such a relief when a large project would come in, and we could quickly mobilize a highly motivated, experienced team to meet the job's needs.

One time, after a long stint without work, cash was getting low. I decided to take money out of my personal retirement account to keep the business running. The work still didn't come. I curtailed my paycheck. Cash continued to dwindle.

There was a limit to what we could support, and we needed a new solution to our cash flow situation. Deborah came up with a furlough system. The furlough enabled us to keep health insurance benefits for our people but stopped their paychecks. We presented it to our teams. They understood the situation and welcomed it. Some took odd jobs. Others took vacations.

Then, shortly after, we had a break with one of the largest US phone companies. They were planning a very large project. We proposed that we could support their national needs, demonstrating how our team had the experience and could mobilize almost overnight. That was enough to convince them. Within six weeks, we had more than 125 people supporting the project across the United States.

We experienced miracles like that all the time. Over the years, we stuck together. We celebrated marriages and babies and even mourned the deaths of some of our members. We did it all together, and eventually we grew into one of the world's largest microwave integration companies.

Not all my decisions were good ones, and that included some bad personnel choices.

We had reached a high point as a company. Our reputation as a microwave integrator was at its peak. I was getting tired, and I needed someone to take my place. We were in the greatest growth year we had ever experienced, working in eight different countries on half a dozen large projects.

I was searching for someone to lead the operations, and I lost focus on what mattered most to our success. Instead of selecting an individual who promoted our culture, I wanted someone with a pedigree of corporate management. Someone who led large organizations. Had the educational credentials I thought necessary to guide us through the next phase.

I was introduced to Richard. He had an MBA and a degree in finance. He knew structure and strategy, and he had been in a leadership position at another very large company. I was looking for his kind of experience, thinking that was what we needed. I assumed taking care of our people was understood. After all, Richard was very nice. He had a great family with good kids and a very supportive wife. I figured that must have been how he managed people too.

I provided the technical orientation Richard needed to take over our operations, but I paid little attention to how he managed people. The transition took time, and as Richard came up to speed, I transitioned out of daily management. As Richard took more control, our most important asset—our people—started to leave. With the staff departures came revenue losses.

It was gradual at first. Then, over the next year, the pace of decline quickened. Some people were comfortable with Richard's style and the culture he created, so I reasoned that the staff who were leaving were probably not performing. I figured Richard was just finding the inefficiencies.

Then one day I got a call from someone not afraid to share their unhappiness with the new regime. I had an open-door policy, and everyone knew they could share openly with me. Not everyone took me up on this, but on that day, I heard it. Loud and clear. How did I miss this? I thought as I heard the frightening stories. Richard had never shown that kind of behavior with me.

We were in trouble, and I had no one but myself to blame. In my quest to act like a big, grownup company, I completely missed the most important element of the most successful companies.

Jim Collins explained it in *Good to Great*, his *New York Times* bestseller detailing the results from one of the most comprehensive research studies ever conducted about corporate success. Patrick Lencioni wrote about it in not one book but several, making Lencioni one of the most sought-after corporate consultants of the day.

But I missed it. The single most important component of our success was empathy for our people and a culture of care. I knew I had to address the situation, but I worried. Was I too late? I had lost more than half of the team, including key people who had helped make us what we were.

Of course, I decided to let Richard go, but in the end, he ended up doing it himself. Our dwindling revenue and thinning staff created a less successful company—one Richard wasn't interested in being involved with. It wasn't long before he tendered his resignation. I respectfully thanked him, and as he walked out, I set about cleaning up the mess.

It took another decade before we put ourselves back on solid ground, but the lesson learned was invaluable. (Yet another Harvard MBA for me!)

Chouinard understood this principle and grew Patagonia into not only one of the best places to work in America, but also a business enjoying sustainable success decade after decade. Collins and Lencioni knew it, making the delivery of that message their life's work. I knew it...and forgot it...and then remembered it.

The most important asset of any company is its people, and the only way to build teams that work effectively together is to provide an empathetic place for employees to work. A place where they feel welcome and supported.

Put your people first. It's a deceptively simple but effective formula.

About Marty

Marty Snyder is a business leader with a track record of success in founding and advising companies in telecommunications and energy infrastructure development. Mr. Snyder's primary experience is in devising strategies and frameworks for executing large-scale projects. His expertise includes technology identification, system development, budgeting, and fostering a motivating work culture to drive project completion. A keen observer of human behavior, he specializes in cultivating productive company cultures that align with objectives, earning recognition from clients and colleagues for his supportive work environments that empower teams to overcome challenges.

Having consulted with prominent corporations like GTE Mobilnet, Pacific Bell Mobile Services, ALLTEL, and AT&T, Marty has overseen strategy, planning, engineering, and the development of over $3 billion in wireless infrastructure. As a co-founder of three enterprises, he contributed to culture creation, business development, and operational leadership, driving over $300 million in revenue. Mr. Snyder led the development of three innovative software applications, enhancing data collection accuracy and engineering efficiency while reducing costs.

Presently, Marty is dedicated to reducing greenhouse gas emissions by improving energy storage systems. Collaborating with industry leaders, he is committed to developing cutting-edge energy storage technology aimed at generating 3,000 Megawatt hours of storage within five years. His diverse experience in infrastructure projects has honed his ability to synthesize disparate components, overcoming conflicts to achieve successful outcomes. Mr. Snyder's four decades of project development across varied contexts have equipped him with universal principles for systematic, successful problem-solving adaptable to any industry.

Notably, Mr. Snyder played a role in the development of GTE Mobilnet's statewide cellular system in Hawaii. A founding member of Reliant Ventures, Inc., he provided management consulting to wireless operators, later founding CIC, a premier wireless deployment and integration company. Under his leadership, CIC became a global leader in Microwave Integration, and developing a software system PathDesigner automating microwave engineering.

Currently serving as President and CEO of SuperCap Energy LLC, Marty Snyder drives the mission to establish 3,000 MWh of renewable energy storage within five years. Leading in supercapacitor-based energy storage systems, SuperCap Energy facilitates large-scale reduction of greenhouse gases at an affordable cost. These supercapacitors enhance renewable energy efficiency by safely storing and discharging energy during peak demand, providing grid stability and regulation. With unmatched durability, supercapacitors outperform other energy storage technologies in both environmental impact and cost-effectiveness

CHAPTER 5

HELPING OTHERS: A WIN-WIN IN BUSINESS

BY DAN MCKENZIE

Just weeks before a skateboard invitational was to be held at the Derby Downs in Akron, Ohio, in 1977, I called the producers of CBS Sports Spectacular—a big sports anthology program—and asked if I could participate.

"What is it that you do?" the producer asked, with a hint of skepticism.

"I'm going to do a handstand on my skateboard the whole way down the derby track," I replied.

"You've got to be kidding me," he said.

I wasn't. Even though I hadn't seen the track yet, I was confident I could pull it off.

When I showed up to demonstrate for them what I could do and attempt to qualify for the event, the producer cleared the track. I had no idea what I was getting into. The hill's slope was daunting. The elite of the skate world, all hailing from the golden coasts of California, got ready 989 feet up the hill, almost three-quarters the way to the top. They would rip down the track at unimaginable speeds, attempting to not get thrown off their boards and crash.

When it was my turn, I ambitiously decided to climb further up the hill, to the top, over 1,000 feet up the track. The track was much taller, much faster, than anything I had ever attempted before, but I got up on the board in my handstand and started down. That track was fast, and as I picked up speed, up to thirty miles per hour, I realized the smooth track made it that much faster.

As I approached the bottom of the hill, my speed significant, the other skateboarders greeted my run with a standing ovation and a big round of applause. I was in.

And it was then that I, Handstandan, was learning the importance of empathy. You get a sense of how it's hitting them. You get a lot of sensory feedback: "I'm doing something good. I'm making people happy." It felt good.

AVIATION BUSINESS TAKES OFF

Years later, as I started out in business, I continued seeking that positive reaction from people. To this day, in everything I do in business, I like to help people, solve habitual problems, make their lives easier. It has all led to growth in my businesses. But in every instance, that hasn't come without a complete team effort. I've had great people as part of my teams. All of my companies have had very talented individuals, and we all share the same goal of what we're trying to get done. And when you have that shared goal, you pick up speed on getting your results.

An example is when I worked in the aviation industry, a company that leased jets to airlines around the world was desperately seeking to get long-range navigation systems installed. The big companies that did this type of work were backlogged, so I saw it as an opportunity to get my foot in the door, though my company, Aircraft Systems & Manufacturing (ASM), was tiny. While the closest competitor said it would take them thirty days per aircraft, we said we could do it in four days.

Naturally, the owner was skeptical. So we told him he wouldn't owe us a dime if we couldn't deliver—but if we could, I said, we wanted to do their entire fleet. We got all their aircraft. We solved a problem for him and got to grow our company as a result. ASM achieved the fastest, highest quality and lowest costs in the aviation community for these types of aircraft modifications.

I always worked hard to understand and empathize with what customers wanted and needed, and to provide them the solutions they needed. What did that focus on efficiency and customer service get me? First and foremost, we developed an excellent reputation. Anyone can tell you that goes a really long way when it comes to getting ahead.

We received glowing letters of recommendation, and the word spread about the quality of work we did for companies, always providing them more than they expected.

EXPECTING NOTHING IN RETURN— BUT GAINING MUCH

Another example from when I was working in aviation is when I got a phone call one afternoon from a man with a heavy accent, asking if I would come to Jordan to fix the king's private airplane. I was considered very knowledgeable in long-range navigation systems, and he requested my expertise. I don't know how much more flattering you can get than getting a call from the king of a country to come fix his private airplane!

After I fixed it, I was told his majesty wanted to know how much he owed me. My answer was, "Nothing." I told them they had treated me like royalty the whole time, and more importantly, I felt bad that he had already paid to have it fixed before from another US-based company, and it didn't work. So I was happy to do it gratis. That's a glowing example of being empathetic to someone even with loads of power and money.

Then, word of mouth proved to be powerful. In the aviation industry, especially corporate jets, if your reputation is decent, you're 'gonna' get a lot of recommendations from word of mouth. This all led to me being able to provide my expertise to many other successful and powerful people, all who owned their own private jets, and to travel all over the world. Celebrities, Fortune 500 companies, and sports figures all benefited from the residue of my empathy.

I got to meet a lot of really cool people. I got to meet former race car driver Mario Andretti; singer-songwriter John Denver; Jack Nicklaus, retired professional golfer and golf course designer; Nick Caporella, chairman and CEO of National Beverage Corp., and many others. I did long-range navigation work, an advanced technology in high demand, on each of their airplanes. This also led to doing similar work for companies that leased out planes for charter flights.

ULTIMATE EMPATHY FOR THE PLANET

After my career in aviation, I started another company with a much more ambitious goal of focusing on global environmental issues. Memios LLC, as with my past businesses, set out to solve problems not only for businesses but also for the masses—but we had much more audacious goals than my previous challenges. This time, the problem was waste management.

We started by understanding the problem for hospitals. To keep patient products hygienic and bacteria-free, the hospitals produce a large amount of waste. Their current waste removal methods, however, are slow, labor-intensive, and come with a myriad of other problems. The work is usually performed by a staff of people lumbering in already congested hallways and taking up valuable elevator space while slowly moving push carts from point A to point B. Memios provided a solution with more efficient, effective, and automated waste removal technology.

Currently, our technology is being used in some of the most prestigious hospitals in the country, including:

- MD Anderson Cancer Center
- Duke University Medical Center in Durham, North Carolina
- Massachusetts General Hospital (the third-oldest hospital in the United States) in Boston
- Jackson Memorial Hospital (one of the largest federally-funded hospitals in the U.S.A.) in Miami
- Atrium Health
- Ohio State University - Wexner Medical Center in Columbus, Ohio

So far, it has proved to be a win-win.

Staff members put the trash in our load stations, and the automated system takes the trash to the central collection area via a totally sealed underground piping network at speeds of thirty meters per second. Once the trash is put into the loading points, no one is exposed to it again—not patients, not staff. This saves the hospital significant money, time, and labor.

Here is what is exciting: We are able to move the trash ten times cheaper, ten times faster, and with ten times better quality. We're truly providing solutions that are ten times better than what they're currently doing. We're trying to help them save money and save time without compromising quality. That's our driving force, all being led by empathy.

On large hospital campuses, we're typically moving twenty tons of trash every six to eight hours! It also cuts down on intangible issues such as staff back, shoulder, and neck injuries. This fixes a lot of issues for the clients. And we can see we are coming to an inflection point where the industry we're creating is about to take off.

Our goal now is to bring this technology to other venues as well as neighborhoods. Imagine no garbage trucks needing to enter neighborhoods and all residential waste for a neighborhood being picked up off-site in one central location. Here's how it works: Homeowners would put their trash—including recyclables—in waste stations in their garages, and it would be transported through a sealed-pipe network within thirty seconds.

This would greatly reduce carbon emissions because trucks—that get just two to three miles per gallon—wouldn't be starting and stopping at every house. The early morning routine is familiar wherever you go. They pull up to the curb in front of your house, pick up the load you left out, then drive a little farther to pick up the next one. It is the ultimate definition of inefficiency. That happens in every neighborhood in nearly every city. We're not just talking about inefficiency on a national basis, but a global one.

And our system eliminates the noise, odors, and road congestion while greatly reducing greenhouse gasses.

Would this solution scare off the current waste management companies? We've listened to what those companies want. They, like anyone else, are on the hunt for more efficient and effective solutions that positively affect their bottom line. We have that solution.

This is the ultimate empathy for the planet and people.

EMPATHY: THE NEXT GENERATION

Over time, I have had many opportunities to share with individuals the importance of empathy. I've been approached many times and asked how I've been able to be successful in business, travel the world (I've been to 126 countries), and meet interesting and prominent people. And I'm happy to share that with them. When they ask, it opens the door to teaching them, in addition to daily leading by example.

I like to share that there are three things that are a must in business—that success comes down to being first, being different, or being the best. I share the importance of being able to focus on goals and tune out all the noise in the busy, modern world we live in.

So many people want to own their own businesses, and they are willing to work hard, but they're so inundated with noise that they can't focus clearly—which leaves them feeling lost or overwhelmed. What do I mean by noise? Anything that isn't part of their goal—you have to focus on achieving your goal. In business, you can't let the news, social media, texts, sound bites, and so on overwhelm your mind. When you can clearly focus, it's so much easier to achieve your goals.

These principles have served me well, whether skateboarding, fixing aircraft, or implementing hygienic and environmentally friendly waste-removal technologies.

Wherever my business takes me down the road, what I learned as Handstandan all those years ago, in addition to these proven business principles, will go along with me—empathizing with and genuinely seeking to help others will continue to drive me toward success.

About Dan

Dan McKenzie has always been driven by an unyielding spirit of learning and growth. As a young enthusiast, he shattered records in skateboarding, notably by innovating his own hydraulic braking system in the 1970s that enabled him to manage the speed and control of the skateboards while riding them on his hands. Featured on CBS Sports Spectacular, his invention allowed him to set unprecedented distance and speed records, casting him into the spotlight of the extreme sports community.

Beyond skateboarding, McKenzie's innate curiosity steered him towards international business and aviation. Demonstrating an astute understanding of diverse cultures, intricate business frameworks, and cutting-edge technology, he became an indispensable troubleshooter in the aviation sector. His expertise proved invaluable to major airlines and corporate aircraft owners globally, tackling intricate flight deck avionics systems and creating strict standards for regulatory compliance.

Harnessing this rich reservoir of knowledge and expertise, McKenzie founded Aircraft Systems & Manufacturing, Inc. (ASM). As CEO, he transformed the company into an industry trailblazer, pioneering outsourced engineering services and aircraft modifications. His revolutionary business strategies not only slashed operational costs, but also propelled ASM to achieve one of the highest profit margins in the aviation community.

Beyond the corporate realm, McKenzie, having traveled to 126 countries and countless international and domestic cities, nurtured an insatiable drive for global impact. His extensive travels only fueled his passion for environmental and humanitarian causes. This led him to establish Memios, LLC, introducing groundbreaking high pressure pneumatic transport systems for municipal solid waste. Within a decade, Memios was hailed as the world's leading high-tech waste management system, topping unprecedented performance metrics.

Today, as a revered entrepreneur, McKenzie sheds light on pivotal market dynamics, technological advancements, and strategies for growth. His legacy is a testament to his roles as a boundary-pushing skateboarder, aviation business executive, and visionary entrepreneur. In every chapter of his life, McKenzie has epitomized the essence of an empathic leader, leaving an indelible imprint on the world.

Connect with Dan:

- www.memios.com
- Dan Mckenzie (@DanMckenzie777) / X

- https://www.linkedin.com/company/memios-llc/mycompany/
- https://www.linkedin.com/in/daniel-mckenzie-14090810/
- https://www.youtube.com/watch?v=blVIaHlgVZ4

CHAPTER 6

BREAKFAST WITH LARRY: WHAT I LEARNED FROM THE KING OF INTERVIEWS

BY NICK NANTON

Memorabilia lines the walls of my studio. Each piece is a memory, accumulated over years of waiting outside buses of well-known musicians and hanging out after shows in smoky bars and clubs.

Despite my love of music and years of attempting to break into that industry, one of the most meaningful keepsakes in my collection has nothing to do with music. It's a simple set of suspenders and a necktie. They seem unassuming among the flashier pieces in the collection, but they belonged to none other than the incomparable Larry King.

Pieces from his signature look, they were a gift from Larry's family after his passing. Today, they stand as a physical reminder of all the lessons I took from my interactions with Larry. Lessons about establishing trust, building professional and personal relationships, and leading with empathy.

Many years before, I bought a charity breakfast with author, radio and television host, and interviewer extraordinaire, Larry King. I'm fascinated by people who operate at the top of their industries. As a filmmaker, I routinely interview people, and I wanted the chance to talk to the man who (conservatively) had interviewed over 50,000 people across his radio and television shows.

After making the winning bid, I called Larry's assistant to set up the private breakfast. I was given a date and time to meet him at Nate'n Al's, his favorite deli in Beverly Hills. I arrived, and shortly after, Larry walked through the door. He looked exactly as I expected. The delicatessen smelled of its signature corned beef hash and lox, and Larry was as comfortable there as someone strolling into their own living room.

After the introductions and pleasantries, he told me he'd been having breakfast at this deli every day he was in town for more than forty years. It was as good as home to him. He also told me his friends always met him there. Rain or shine. Even though this was meant to be a private breakfast, he knew they would still come.

And, true to Larry's word, they did. Several beloved, celebrated actors and TV personalities filtered in and joined us at our booth.

Among the noisy deli chatter, Larry leaned across the table and asked me, "How can I help?"

That's where he started the conversation. He immediately respected that I'd paid for this opportunity, and he was going to commit to the process.

I told him the three things I hoped to get out of the time.

- One, he'd done more interviews than probably anyone else in the world. As an interviewer myself, I wanted the chance to talk to him about that process.

- Two, I knew he had incredible stories. I just wanted to hear some of the amazing anecdotes he had gathered over the decades.

- And three, if there happened to be an opportunity to work together down the line, great.

Over breakfast, we talked about Larry's favorite interviews. Having talked to everyone from Martin Luther King and Jackie Robinson to Mikhail Gorbachev and every sitting US president since Gerald Ford, he was hard-pressed to pick a favorite.

The stories were incredible and seemingly unlimited. I was enthralled. After our breakfast, I asked if he'd be open to talking to me about sharing his life story. He was, and he handed over his cell phone number and house line.

"I'm a communicator," he said, looking me straight in the eye. "Don't text. Call me." I went off to put my proposal together, and I FedExed everything shortly after to his assistant.

In the intervening weeks, I called Larry several times. (Without fail, these interactions always started out the same. He'd answer. I'd say it was Nick Nanton. He'd say, "Who?" I'd give him more context, and he'd warmly reply, "Oh! Hello, Nick!")

Ultimately, it turned out a friend of Larry was already promised the opportunity to cover his life story. At the time, I was filming Rudy Ruettiger's documentary, and I immediately called Larry back. (It's Nick Nanton. Who?...)

I asked him if he'd be willing to go on an Internet TV show instead and be interviewed by me about his life. When Larry agreed, I got to work creating the show, which didn't yet exist, and then booking a time for Larry to come on.

After that interview, I knew we had captured something really special. I sent it to my editor and told him this needed to be made into a documentary.

After the editing, I once again called Larry. (It's Nick Nanton. Who?...) I told him what we'd been working on and asked if I could show it to him. He invited me to his house for a viewing.

I waited anxiously in his study for hours as a technician came onsite to rewire the television. (Apparently Larry's sons had disconnected the TV from his extremely complicated system to plug in their Xbox and enjoy some late-night play with friends.) Once the technical issues were finally resolved, the documentary began to play.

Throughout the viewing, I just watched Larry watching the piece. He laughed at parts. He got misty-eyed at others. When the credits rolled, he barely took a beat. "Excellent. Excellent work!" he said. "Now what are we going to do with it?"

With his blessing, we got to work on distribution. After putting together a simple one-page deal, Larry signed and came onto the project as an executive producer. We ended up doing one season of the show, *In Case You Didn't Know*, and the final product earned us both an Emmy.

LESSONS FROM LARRY

My time with Larry gifted me with many lessons about business and trust. Because we both approached the initial relationship with empathy and respect, we were ultimately able to create something impactful, lasting, and successful together.

- **Building a real relationship takes time.**

When I met Larry for breakfast at that Beverly Hills deli, we didn't know each other at all. We had no mutual friends or connections.

We developed our genuine relationship through empathy. We both took steps to lay the foundation for mutual trust, understanding, and respect.

That step-by-step approach allowed us to drive toward a relationship that wasn't superficial, and it ended up producing fruitful, powerful, creative results.

- **Don't overstep.**

Building trust means understanding where the other person is coming from and operating in a way that respects that.

When I first met Larry, I didn't try to get him to commit to working together at that meeting. He wasn't in a place yet where he liked, knew, or trusted me. The ask would have been a major overstep at that point in our relationship. Beyond that, it would have certainly hurt my chances of getting to a point where we could ever work together.

Later, after we'd cut together the documentary, which was beyond the scope of what we had discussed, I made sure to get Larry's green light before pursuing the project any further. Releasing anything without his overt permission would have been another major overstep.

Had I overstepped at any point, those decisions would have conveyed a lack of respect that hurt the relationship moving forward.

- **Building trust sometimes requires a bit of creativity.**

The path to working with Larry wasn't an easy straight shot. I had to pivot and adjust, responding to obstacles as they presented themselves throughout the deal.

When the opportunity to work on his life story was denied, I had to figure out what new door I wanted to walk through. That mindset takes two things: creativity and resilience.

But when you give God elbow room, great and unexpected things often happen.

Even if I didn't know exactly how the project would manifest, I knew I wanted to tell Larry's story. My willingness to be creative and persistent created those avenues that allowed the relationship to continue. Without that, the project we ended up creating together never would have come to life.

- **Successful relationship-building requires three keys.**

According to a mentor of mine, Dan Sullivan, the way to make it big comes down to three basic keys.

1. Show up on time.
2. Do what you say you're going to do.
3. Say please and thank you.

Through all my business ventures, I've found these rules for success to be extremely accurate. If you can clear those three hurdles, people are more inclined to like and trust you. You can gain incredible credibility, and that opens so many doors.

The reason each of these keys works so well comes down to empathy.

Showing up on time is a way to signal respect to the other person. You're not going to make them wait around or wonder if the appointment is still happening. Larry and I both showed up to that deli on time, and keeping that appointment was a way for both of us to show respect to the other.

Doing what you say makes you a credible, trustworthy person. Anyone interacting with you (personally or professionally) doesn't have to wonder if you're being genuine or if your intentions are good. Following through the first time is a way to lay that foundation of trust. (I told Larry I'd follow up after our breakfast meeting, and I did.) Continuing to follow up on all your promises and intentions strengthens that trust and respect. Eventually, you become known as someone whose word means something.

Saying please and thank you is a way both to offer respect and to express gratitude. Whenever I was dealing with Larry, his management team, or his family, I was always polite and respectful. I never acted as if I was owed anything, and I was grateful for every opportunity I was given in that relationship.

I make it a point to do this with everyone. I just feel it's the way people should be treated.

When Larry passed away on January 23, 2021, and his family ended up sending me those suspenders and necktie, that was incredibly meaningful. It was a lovely gesture, and it was confirmation that my politeness and respect toward the entire family hadn't gone unnoticed.

- **Highly successful people are relentlessly curious.**

I haven't interviewed nearly as many as Larry, but I have sat down and talked to a lot of people over the years. Every single highly successful person I've talked to has said the same thing drives their success: relentless curiosity.

I have an abundance of respect for anyone who has mastered anything. Whatever the field, I simply respect mastery.

My main reason for wanting to meet Larry King was my own curiosity. He was the absolute master of interviewing, and I wanted to learn what I could directly from him.

- **Empathy isn't a robotic formula.**

Building trust with someone requires you to approach a relationship with genuine empathy, and that isn't about checking a series of boxes.

You can't get to an empathetic place just by taking a formulaic set of steps. There is no coverall framework for how to build a solid relationship in every situation.

All you can do is actively and genuinely respect the other person. Ensure every action you take considers how it will affect that other person.

Say I had released the King documentary without Larry's permission. Or I had been rude to his family. Or I had acted in our meetings as if Larry owed me something.

Doing any one of those things would have eroded trust and destroyed that relationship—along with any potential future opportunities that connection would have produced.

When you approach a relationship with authentic empathy, the other person can sense that. It doesn't feel forced or contrived.

- **Leave your ulterior motives at the door.**

Did I hope meeting Larry King would lead to some interesting, lucrative projects? Absolutely.

But that didn't mean I went into the relationship with any preconceived notions or constantly had that singular goal in my mind.

A major part of being empathetic is not seeing relationships as transactional. It's not always about what the other person can do for you or what you need from them.

As Larry and I got to know each other better, opportunities presented themselves. I was persistent about following up, but the project gained traction and moved forward because Larry felt the relationship we'd developed wasn't just about what I hoped to gain from him.

- **Your point of view isn't the only point of view.**

Leading with empathy means seeing things from another point of view. It's understanding what motivates others and then tailoring your actions to accommodate.

I knew maintaining my relationship with Larry required me to lead with respect. I had to honor what his manager said, and I had to make sure to show him every creative asset first. If I did that, Larry would feel seen and respected, and the door wouldn't close on those future opportunities.

How Can I Help?

Larry could have never showed up to that deli. He could have been hours late. He could have spent the whole meal chatting with his friends and ignoring me.

But he didn't.

He acknowledged I had paid for this opportunity, and he immediately showed me empathy and respect.

How can I help? That was the first question he asked me.

And because I showed him empathy and respect in return, I ended up gaining a mentor, a partner on what became an Emmy Award–winning series, and a dear friend.

Today, his suspenders and necktie hang framed on my wall among the music memorabilia of my younger years, and when I look at them, I can still hear his deep baritone voice asking me that deeply empathetic question:

HOW CAN I HELP?

About Nick

From the slums of Port au Prince, Haiti, with special forces raiding a sex-trafficking ring and freeing children, to the Virgin Galactic Space Port in Mojave with Sir Richard Branson, the 22-Time Emmy Award Winning Director/Producer, Nick Nanton, has become known for telling stories that connect. Why? Because he focuses on the most fascinating subject in the world: PEOPLE.

As a storyteller and Best-Selling Author, Nick has shared his message with millions of people through his documentaries, speeches, blogs, lectures, and bestselling books. Nick's book *StorySelling* hit *The Wall Street Journal* Best-Seller list and is available on Audible as an audio book. Nick has directed more than 60 documentaries and a sold out Broadway Show (garnering 43 Emmy nominations in multiple regions and 22 wins), including:

- *DREAM BIG: Rudy Ruettiger LIVE on Broadway*
- *Visioneer: The Peter Diamandis Story*
- *Rudy Ruettiger: The Walk On*
- *Operation Toussaint*
- *The Rebound*

Nick has shared the stage, co-authored books, and made films featuring:

- Larry King
- Dick Vitale
- Kenny Chesney
- Charles Barkley
- Coach Mike Krzyzewski
- Jack Nicklaus
- Tony Robbins
- Steve Forbes
- will.i.am
- Sir Richard Branson
- Dean Kamen
- Ray Kurzweil
- Lisa Nichols
- Peter Diamandis
      ......and many more

Nick specializes in bringing the element of human connection to every viewer, no matter the subject. He is currently directing and hosting the series: *In Case You Didn't Know* (Season 1 Executive Produced by Larry King), featuring legends in the worlds of business, entrepreneurship, personal development, technology, and sports.

CHAPTER 7

EMPATHY CREATES COMPANY CULTURE

BY BILL GALLAGHER

There was a heaviness to the air, like most days, as the humidity is legendary. I remember the smell of the marsh, the uneasiness in my stomach, as well as the excitement and anticipation of training day. I'd been on the island for six weeks and it was my recruit training platoon's turn at the gas chamber and the famed Holberton Tower.

Holberton Tower is the rappelling tower located at Marine Corps Recruit Depot Parris Island. It stands above the pine trees and, even for those who don't suffer from a fear of heights, it proves to be intimidating. The opportunity for an adrenaline rush is one of the many reasons I enlisted in the Marines; however, I received much more from the United States Marine Corps than I will ever be able to give back.

One of the main tenets of empathy in leadership is putting yourself in the shoes of those you are leading and demonstrating that you have executed the task at hand or at least tried to understand what it is like. Don't ask someone to do something you haven't done or aren't willing to do yourself. The instructors at MCRD Parris Island embodied this behavior as I witnessed them demonstrating everything they asked the recruits to do (and doing it much better and more efficiently). I watched with admiration as these instructors demonstrated how to tie their own rappelling harness and then execute the drill off the simulated 'helo' platform. They weren't just telling us to do this terrifying task; they were showing us, putting themselves at some level of risk as well. As a very impressionable eighteen-year-old, these qualities forged my own beliefs about leadership. There are many ways to lead. However, demonstrating empathy is one of the keys to great leadership.

Before going too far into my story, I want to share a time when I did *not* practice the skills of empathy. Years had passed from my days as a Marine, and I'd just been newly minted as a CEO. I was participating in a sales call with a former colleague who introduced me to a very desirable potential client. The stakeholder was a VP responsible for data at a large, well-known institution. I was very familiar with the subject matter but brought along a colleague who was a solid closer in this space. I had the pitch down pat, confidently walked in, sat down, and started talking. After 30 minutes, the client stopped me and said, "Bill, I get it. You hire great people and you've got a great company. But how are you going to solve my problem? Do you even know what my problem is?"

It was a 'deer in the headlights' moment, and we lost the opportunity. This is a case study in what not to do. I let my ego and hubris get in the way of my ability to be empathetic toward this potential client. I had access to insiders who could have provided insight, but was too caught up in winning the deal to even position myself to exercise empathy. I tried to solve the problem without really understanding the needs of the client, and unfortunately the deal blew up in my face...and cost my firm a couple million bucks. This was the last time I allowed my ego to get the best of me, at least in terms of sales.

It wasn't like I didn't have leaders who modeled empathy for me. My grandfather had empathy skills as deep as the day is long. Preston had a 10th grade education and lived in an era when people didn't talk much about how to improve their communication skills. His talent as a storyteller allowed him to connect naturally with people. A World War II combat veteran, he grew up poor and during one of the darkest times in our country's history - the Great Depression. He had a great deal of influence over forming my thoughts as I spent summers with him and my grandmother on their South Carolina farm.

When I was 12, I told my grandfather I wanted this expensive fishing rod. My grandfather believed in never spending money on things that weren't vital to survival. Many may have said I was being frivolous and dismissed my young aspirations. He could have told me to use one of the rods in the barn. Instead, he shared a story about a time, after he'd come back from the war, when he'd wanted a certain deer-hunting rifle. He certainly didn't have the money to pay for it, so he decided to figure out a way to earn some extra cash.

They lived on a farm that produced vegetables as well as tobacco. The farm had barns used to dry and cure the crop. He had the idea of drying the hulls from other crops, which made them highly flammable, and selling them to local manufacturers to use as fuel in fire boilers. The first two factories declined, but the third agreed to buy the hulls, and he made enough money to purchase that deer rifle. Instead of dismissing me altogether, he put himself in my shoes and understood my young boy's plight.

His story motivated me. How could I convert the trash around the farm to energy that someone would pay for? Eventually, I had the idea to take the over-ripe fruits and vegetables used for compost and sell them to farmers to feed their livestock. It didn't take long to make enough to buy my fishing rod. My grandfather remembered what it felt like to want something he couldn't afford. That's when I first remember being the recipient of empathy.

I was on the receiving end of empathy again many years later, after graduating from college. I got several job offers but a smaller consulting company offered me five grand more than the others, and I took it. Unfortunately, the CEO had hired 500 of us in a short span of time, and within 18 months, had to lay us all off. He communicated this news by having us dial in to a 1-800-number and listen to a recorded message. That guy never made it on the cover of Empathy Magazine. His ego and thirst for growth at any cost not only damaged his business but also his reputation.

I went back to the companies that had offered me a job 18 months earlier and groveled for an opportunity. I interviewed with one of the partners at Arthur Andersen—this was before the name was synonymous with Enron. He wanted to know why I'd gone with the other firm 18 months earlier. "Why was that $5,000 so important?" I don't know any 20-something year old who wouldn't have found $5,000 important, but

I also had my first child on the way. He intently listened to me and reminisced about his own start in consulting many years prior.

He needed consultants and he liked my story, so he started me that day and matched my previous salary. This busy man who was running a $100 million business got to know a potential employee who he wouldn't even work with directly. That left a huge impression on me and further forged my belief that empathy is foundational to good leadership.

COMPANY CULTURE MATTERS

As a CEO, I try to mimic what was modeled for me. It doesn't matter how busy I am, I try to take time to get to know somebody, especially if I see they're in need. Our company is highly collaborative and familial, and we try to take care of one another. It is worth sacrificing revenue to preserve that culture. Leaders who don't understand that mentality have likely never hit rock bottom. Once they've been bit, gotten sued or fired because they said or did something stupid, then they'll see that money is not everything in business.

You may be wondering how I can afford to put culture over revenue. Sure, I've got shareholders who want a return on their investment, but those shareholders are also employees, so they understand the value of the culture. I'm not working for a Wall Street behemoth solely focused on finances.

Having said that, we need to make money to support our families and the business while continuing to grow. It's a balancing act. We make a conscious decision about what's important, whether it's a client we've got to rush off and see, or an employee who needs help with a particular issue. When we focus on preserving the culture, the money flows. If we chase the dollar, we make stupid decisions. If you have the luxury of focusing on the people with whom you work, and make sure they're taken care of, the money comes.

ARE YOU SELF-AWARE?

Your employees are not going to trust you if you are a leader who isn't aware of how you treat others or how others view you. I once had an employee who was a notorious micromanager. I decided it was time to do 360 feedback, a process of asking the person to request an evaluation from their direct reports on the strengths and weaknesses of their leadership.

I wasn't going to ask someone to do something I wasn't willing to do myself, so first I asked my direct reports, which included this person, to evaluate me. Afterward, I met with this person and said, "You had the opportunity to give me feedback, now I'd like you to do this with your own team." Feedback goes a long way in proving to the un-self-aware person of just how hard it is to work for them. It's not punishment, it's an opportunity for growth. After the evaluation, I could see this employee was more aware of their shortcomings and was trying to make changes.

Company culture is an important part of a business's success. Encouraging our leaders to continue developing soft skills like listening, humility, and showing empathy builds trust with team members, clients, and management. In the Marine Corps, we'd talk about who we wanted in the fighting hole with us. People who'd proven themselves to be credible and trustworthy. Make no mistake, empathy is not weakness or being agreeable with everyone. You will deliver tough messages. However, leading with empathy proves that you can be trusted to weigh the personal impact against the overall goal and choose what's best.

I've also been on the receiving end of decisions made by leaders who hadn't considered how their behavior impacted their team. I left Arthur Andersen after the Enron debacle and went to work for a consulting company that had a 'different' (I'm being generous here) work culture. I was splitting time between two clients, one East Coast, one West Coast. We were replacing much of the East Coast client's manufacturing process software as well as their systems supporting order to cash. This process was described as attempting to perform a heart and lung transplant while the patient is running a marathon. Suffice to say, the project was complex and had huge implications for the success of the client.

Two hundred business and technology strategists and consultants, including myself, were on location for the East Coast client when the partner in charge asked the team to work overtime to make a tight deadline. Their shareholders were all over the board members, the board was all over the CEO, and the CEO was all over everybody else. We agreed to stay two consecutive weekends and not go home. I had a three-year-old at the time, so it's no understatement to say my wife wasn't happy.

On Saturday afternoon, I needed a decision on something I didn't have the authority to make, so I began looking for the partner who had insisted we stay over the weekend. We were in Rochester, New York, in a building that spanned multiple city blocks. Project teams were everywhere. I couldn't locate the manager, so I called his cell phone and each time it went to voicemail. Two hours later, he returned my call and it sounded like he was standing in a wind tunnel. As I tried to explain what I needed, he yelled into the phone, "I can't hear you--I'm on my boat in Fort Lauderdale, and it's windy!"

He probably got his position because he's really good at sales. But as a leader, he sucked. Within three weeks I had another job. When a leader loses credibility, they've lost their employees' trust. I was determined never to make this mistake in my leadership journey.

ADVICE TO YOUNG LEADERS

I learned so much by working for leaders who were good at some things and not so good at other things. After thirty years in business leadership, I'll share a few of the most valuable lessons that, had I known, would have saved me a lot of conflict and hassle.

1. **Lead by example.** Don't ask an employee to do something you aren't willing to do yourself.
2. **Try to remove the emotion from decision-making.**
3. **Check your ego and your biases at the door.** There's nothing worse than an arrogant leader. They may be effective, and a lot of them are billionaires, but they're hard to deal with.
4. **Establish a company culture.** What message are you telegraphing to employees about what's most important?
5. **You are not the smartest person in the room.** I've made a career out of surrounding myself with smarter people and leveraging them to help achieve a goal.

6. **Be the leader you want to be known for.** Egotistical leaders may be successful in the short-term, but they aren't respected, and many times, their employees aren't giving them their best.

7. **Listen more than you talk.** There are people who will have better ideas than you, and you need to listen to them. Without jumping to conclusions.

8. **Be firm, but supportive, consistent, and fair in how you deal with people.**
   I can share leadership wisdom because, over my career, I've been the guy with the ego, I've made decisions when I was emotional, I've been hard to deal with. Sometimes I still am! But with the help of strong role models and a heart for people, I recognize there is a better way. That doesn't mean I don't have to tame my instincts at times, but, overall, if people find you relatable and not arrogant, you'll be more effective at getting things done.

It's easy for me to see the value of empathy. Whether in business or in our personal lives, empathy helps us grow in self-awareness, take accountability for our mistakes, and reminds us we don't have all the answers. With employees, empathy promotes a culture that builds trust and inspires people to give their best. Empathy makes us stronger leaders, people well-regarded and respected, people who others want in the fighting hole with them.

About Bill

Bill Gallagher is the CEO for Systems Evolution Incorporated (SEI), a business and technology consulting firm. He has over 25 years of experience in the Business and Technology Consulting Industry serving Fortune 1000 clients. During his eighteen-year tenure at SEI, Bill has served as a consultant, managing director, and now as CEO. His extensive experience with large consultancies, such as Arthur Andersen and KPMG, as well as smaller boutique consulting firms, uniquely prepared him for his responsibilities as CEO. As a Marine Corp Veteran, Bill leads his team with a commitment to company culture and empowers every employee to own their success.

Bill serves on the board of REACH (www.reachga.org). REACH (Realizing Educational Achievement Can Happen) Georgia's mission is to ensure that Georgia's low income, academically promising students have the academic, social, and financial support needed to graduate from high school, access college, and achieve postsecondary success. Bill holds a degree from the University of Georgia.

Bill enjoys spending his free time with his family, rooting for the Georgia Bulldogs, offshore fishing, traveling, or in the gym.

CHAPTER 8

HOW TO WIN AT THE NEGOTIATION TABLE

BY RADIM PAŘÍK

150 million euros were at stake, and I was responsible for negotiating the contract. I was ready for anything. Prepared. I had expert engineers, lawyers, and technicians on my side.

When I walked in the door, the other negotiator immediately approached me. "I hear you're a great negotiator," he said as we shook hands. "I lost a negotiation just this morning with my daughter. I hope you give me a chance." We laughed easily, and I immediately liked him.

After forty-five minutes at the negotiation table, I looked at the deal we'd created. We didn't get any of the results we wanted. The other negotiator was walking away with everything.

It remains the worst contract I've ever negotiated, but throughout the meeting, I felt understood. Seen. It felt as easy as talking to a best friend. I immediately told my assistant to find out everything about this guy. After some digging, it turned out he was a former hostage negotiator in Germany. I didn't recognize it at the time, but he was using hallmarks of the FBI negotiation model (empathy, active listening, mirroring) to steer the negotiation in his favor.

After this interaction, I signed up for my first negotiation course. I put myself on the path that eventually led to becoming the president of the

Association of Negotiators, a Chief Negotiation Officer®, a Certified Global Negotiator®, and the most-cited negotiator in my home country of the Czech Republic.

After studying negotiation under several former FBI agents, at Harvard University, and at the Swiss University of St. Gallen, I founded my own negotiation company. Today, our clients include some of the top international Fortune 500 companies. I'm also the chief advisor for negotiations of the presidential office of the Czech Republic.

Our team today is composed of five specialized negotiators. One employee specifically supports women in tough negotiations, and another focuses on empowering deaf individuals throughout these meetings. Her expertise in body language helps our team read what people are really feeling and thinking throughout the negotiation process.

The team handles a variety of high-stakes international automotive, retail, finance, construction, pharmaceutical, and political deals.

14 KEYS OF A SUCCESSFUL NEGOTIATION

Negotiation is a bit like driving a car. You can have all the instruction in the world, but sitting down behind the wheel teaches you best. As you get into your negotiation cars and start to drive, here are the principles I take into any negotiation room.

1. Never negotiate against someone.

The person on the other side of the negotiation table is not your enemy. If you go into a negotiation with that mentality, you're never going to reach a mutually beneficial solution.

You're negotiating *with* someone. Never *against* them.

Negotiations can be high-stress, high-stakes situations. Everyone is under pressure. It should be clear your task is to help everyone in that room reach a common goal.

Once you start putting arguments on the table, you've lost. An argument means I'm right and you're wrong. That mindset destroys any chance of being allies at the table.

2. Actively listen.

Active listening is a core principle of empathy, and it's critical during any negotiation.

Dive deep into the interests of your counterparty, and be 100 percent focused on the human being on the other side of the table. No negotiation is about the interests, goals, or needs of one person alone.

Active listening requires:

a) **Respect**. You must genuinely want to hear what the other person has to say. Don't interrupt them. Don't minimize or dismiss their point of view. Part of active listening is respecting that you have a different perspective than I do. It's acknowledging we have a conflict we need to resolve, but we can come to that conflict without judgment.

b) **Understanding**. You see things completely different than me. Part of my job is to understand that. Why do you see things differently? What's your motivation?

c) **Acceptance**. Even if you completely disagree with the other person, a good negotiator demonstrates acceptance of that person and their viewpoint. If someone says a point in the contract is problematic, even if I disagree, I accept there's a problem. Why? Because the other person perceives it that way.

d) **Silence**. In a negotiation, if the other person is talking, that's a good sign. You must bring the capability of being silent to any negotiation table.

3. Don't lose your humanity.

A few years back, I was the lead negotiator in an acquisition deal. It involved a 200 million euro contract and the selling of shares in four different European countries.

The negotiator on the other side was a tough, experienced businessman. He was famous in the world of negotiation for getting people into deadlocks. He would refuse to move the deal forward, stealing time until the looming contract deadline caused the other side to give in.

We were nearing that crucial date in our negotiations when we met again. Immediately, I could tell he wasn't focused or concentrating. Suddenly he was saying yes to contractual points he never would have agreed to in previous meetings. My first reaction was delight. I knew we were going to win this hard-fought negotiation.

After two more hours at the table, it became clear something was very wrong. The more I tuned into him, the more I realized he simply wasn't meaningfully present. I interrupted the negotiation and invited him outside. I bought him a coffee, and we walked and talked as we circled the building. Two times. Five times. Ten times.

We talked about strategy and business and the project, and after an hour, I posed the question. "What's going on with you today?" I said. "I can't believe you of all people are so unprepared for this negotiation."

His entire demeanor changed. He confided in me that he'd had an upsetting emergency involving his son the day before. As a father, he was distraught and at a total loss about what to do.

I immediately told him we were canceling the negotiation. I told him to go home, be with his family, and solve the problem. "Your son," I said, "is more important than this meeting."

When we reconvened in three weeks, we were no longer negotiating. It felt like the meeting of two friends. At the end of that negotiation, we ended up building something entirely new together. The deal was bigger and better, and it involved more money and more exciting business possibilities.

To this day, we're good friends. Our families even vacation together.

High-stakes negotiation often involves important matters, lots of money, and tons of risk. Despite that, I always want to prioritize my humanity. If I can see you're not an active partner in our negotiation, it stops being a negotiation. My job at that point is to help you as a fellow human.

4. The zero-sum mentality only works once.

If you approach a negotiation with a zero-sum mentality, you might win that negotiation. But you'll never create long-term relationships. In pursuit of the singular goal, you'll miss the opportunity to create something better for everyone.

I could have pushed that particular negotiation to the end. I could have won in every aspect of that contract. But the result never would have been as good as what we achieved together three weeks later.

When we proceeded on the same side of the table, it opened the door for ongoing, meaningful, productive opportunities.

5. Create a secure base.

I'm ashamed my first thought in that negotiation was about winning. I saw my counterparty wasn't OK, and for a moment, I forgot my primary aim: to create a space that's safe and secure for everyone in the room. This was a massive lesson for me in leadership, negotiation, and empathy.

With trust, it's possible for everyone to be happy with the solution you create together. If the other side actually trusts you, you can achieve great results.

6. Be attuned to the other person.

Paraphrase what others say. Mirror. Label emotions. Deescalate pressure-filled, stressful situations. These tactics are possible when you're truly paying attention to the other side.

When you establish a connection and bond with others during negotiations, you start to genuinely see the situation from a different perspective. Your mind is opened to solutions that everyone can be happy with.

I know these mindsets work because my company has a 95 percent success rate in their negotiations.

7. Be authentic.

The difficult thing about empathy is that no one believes you if you're faking it.

The human limbic system is the oldest program we have. Ten thousand years ago, we used it to sense when something bad was coming. It was a critical survival tool. Today, it means we're finely tuned to recognize when someone is faking interest or feigning a relationship.

If you're not bringing genuine empathy to the table, your actions will do more harm than good.

8. Be collaborative.

A good negotiation never involves giving someone a solution and telling them what they have to do.

If I give you my solution, it's not our solution. Negotiation isn't about being at war with someone. It's not about me only giving or taking. It's about collaboratively developing a solution that works for everyone.

If both sides of the negotiation table didn't need each other, it wouldn't be a negotiation. When I walk into a room, I know both sides need something, and I'm there to help everyone get those things.

Both empathy and negotiation are predicated on reciprocity. Without that, neither will be successful.

9. Be calm.

The hardest negotiations aren't with experienced, tough-as-nails negotiators. It's with the inexperienced.

If you're not used to negotiating, you often enter the deal with stress, multiple triggers, emotional instability, and fear. Fear is the most dangerous emotion in a negotiation. It clouds your judgment and only allows you to see one solution on the other side of the discussions.

In those cases, my job is to be a calming presence that deescalates emotion and creates neutral stability at the table.

10. Be prepared.

In high-stakes negotiations, preparation is crucial. A good 80 percent of your success depends on this. You have to be ready and extremely focused throughout the deal.

This doesn't mean you lose sight of your empathy or the fact you're negotiating with another human being, but you also have to do all your due diligence. Do everything in your power to come to that table as knowledgeable and prepared as possible.

11. Be humble.

Becoming a great negotiator is a lifelong process of learning. I always say I'm not a good negotiator. I'm just on a good path.

The second I think I have nothing left to learn about negotiation is the second I've lost the ability to win at the table.

12. Disagree respectfully.

Having empathy in negotiations doesn't mean I just say yes to whatever the other person wants. Being empathetic means it's not necessary to agree with you. I can have a completely different opinion and still bring deep empathy to our interactions.

What I can't do is disrespect your differing opinion. I must respect the validity of your thoughts, perspectives, and beliefs.

13. Be grateful.

When someone takes the time and energy to meet with me and

explain their opinion on a matter, it doesn't matter if I agree or disagree. I need to be grateful for the energy they put into that interaction. I need to thank them for their input and their effort.

I know I wouldn't be where I am today without the love and support of my colleagues and family. In all my personal and professional pursuits, I bring a mindset of immense gratitude.

14. Leave them with a good last impression.

Everyone talks about the importance of that first impression, but I argue the last impression is even more important. No one will remember how you came. Everyone will remember how you left.

At the end of any negotiation, successful or otherwise, always be respectful. Say thank you. Convey your appreciation for all their hard work and time throughout the process.
A good last impression leaves the door open for those future collaborations and professional relationships.

WHAT MAKES A SUCCESSFUL NEGOTIATION?

At my company, we don't work for quota or profit and loss statements. A negotiation is considered successful when two conditions are met:

- One, we've achieved a result somewhere between the minimum and maximum goal of each side.

- Two, we can meet for a beer afterward to celebrate.

It's not just about the result; it's about the relationships you form.

WHY DOES NEGOTIATION MATTER?

Every summer, I go to a camp for kids without parents, and I teach these children and young adults how to negotiate.

The camp attendees are between sixteen and twenty-one years old, and most have endured unspeakable tragedies in their lives. Knowing how to negotiate unlocks the opportunity for these people to get what they want out of life.

Leadership is a constant negotiation act. If you're able to negotiate empathetically, you can improve conditions and make everyone's life better. When two opposing sides are too far away from each other and no creative solution can be found, that's when we have wars. Physical wars. Financial wars. Court battles.

Every war eventually ends at the negotiation table. By entering into situations with a genuinely empathetic mindset, we can all negotiate more successfully and avoid more of those instances where any two sides feel compelled to go to war in the first place.

About Radim

Radim Pařík is an international professional negotiator, lecturer, senior manager and sign language interpreter. He serves as the president of Association of Negotiators and is a prolific speaker and author featured prominently in Czech Republic's media landscape. Widely cited across television, radio and newspapers, Radim stands as the most accomplished negotiator in the country.

Radim is the acclaimed author of several books including, *Arguments Don't Work – The New Law of Negotiation, Arguments Don't Work – 6:4 is the Minimum, Interviews Before the War,* and *The Art of Negotiating Anything (Umění vyjednat cokoliv)*, which soared to bestseller status within just five weeks of its release. Alongside his literary achievements, he holds membership in the prestigious international Negotiation Club and has an impressive record as a multiple-time Czech Republic and European Karate Champion.

Born in the Czech Republic, Radim's journey has led him across borders. He resided in Germany and subsequently in Poland. In both these nations, he assumed prominent leadership roles within the multinational Schwarz Group, an enterprise that Forbes recognizes as one of the globe's top five largest retailers.

After obtaining his MSc and MBA in Strategic Management from Nottingham Trent University, Radim earned his PhD in Negotiation from LIGS University. He further honed his negotiation skills through training under the guidance of multiple former FBI agents and completed Harvard University's negotiation program, culminating in his graduation from the Harvard Negotiation Master Class. Radim's educational achievements also include graduating from the Certified Global Negotiator program at the University of St. Gallen, as well as mastering negotiation techniques based on Mossad principles.

Radim heads the negotiation program at Tomáš Bata University and collaborates with other institutions. He founded Radim Pařík's Fascinating Academy for commercial negotiation training. A proud disciple of Chris Voss, he is the co-owner of PR PA RT NE RS Advisory Group and initiated the Association of Negotiators, uniting professionals across five countries on four continents.

Radim aids TOP 100 companies in Czech & Slovak Republic for tough negotiations and lectures on negotiations for Security Information Service agents. He earned the Czechoslovak LinkedIn Personality of 2020 and 2022.

Contact Radim at:

- Web: www.fascinating.academy
- Email: fascinujte@fascinating.academy

Social Media

- Facebook: www.facebook.com/radim.parik
- LinkedIn: www.linkedin.com/in/radim-parik
- Instagram: https://www.instagram.com/radimparik/
- Radim Parik (@ParikRadim) / X

CHAPTER 9

A CULTURE TO BELIEVE IN

BY ADAM HAGFORS

COVID CHANGED EVERYTHING

In hindsight, I got the results of the COVID-19 shutdown entirely wrong. At the beginning, I believed that in-home schooling would be a success. I saw the opposite fate in store for remote work. I believed that would fall on its face. Within a matter of months, everyone would be dying to get back to the office. As it turns out, the opposite proved to be true.

The reasoning behind my thinking might have, in hindsight, been sound. I thought that lockdowns would create a unique opportunity for young children, forced to stay inside of their own homes, to learn from a selection of the world's greatest teachers. That sense of optimism turned out to be a bit of 'Pollyanna' thinking.

In my imagination, this scenario sounded ideal. But try telling that to anyone who experienced nearly an entire year locked down in quarantine with a kid at home. There was nothing ideal about the experience. Remote schooling was, for most parents, an ordeal they struggled just to survive.

My pessimism about remote work also proved incorrect. We came to discover that a considerable percentage of the workforce enjoyed working at home; many even thrived under autonomous conditions. Productivity stayed high, creating a dilemma for a lot of employers.

When the time finally came for them to return to their old workplaces, many were reluctant to transition back.

When the COVID-19 lockdowns started in early March 2020, I retreated from the city with the rest of my family. We were fortunate to have a vacation home in the country where we could ride out the worst of what we believed the virus had in store. Spring became summer and, when autumn finally rolled around and the virus came under control, our leaders were confronted with the question of whether to return to the office.

I struggled to know the best direction to take my company. Whether the virus was under control or not, COVID-19 had already disrupted workplace culture. Would remote work decimate it altogether? There was no way we could be sure either way. Ultimately, in October of that year, we made the tough decision. My company decided to go fully remote.

OPPORTUNITIES TO LEARN

I was a different kind of kid. My attraction to the world of money and finance started from a very young age, making my career a truly lifelong pursuit.

Numbers always made a lot of sense to me. I remember subscribing to *Investor's Business Daily* when I was just a kid, seemingly too young to be absorbed with matters of finance. They used to offer a free trial subscription, and since I didn't have any money of my own yet, I remember signing up multiple times in order to keep those issues coming to the house. I must have stood out, immersed in reading about the stock market while other kids on the street were busy playing video games.

Later on, while in High School, I held down an entry level job at an accounting firm. It wasn't an exciting position, but it connected me to the world I knew I wanted to be a part of. Knowing where I wanted to go had a way of narrowing my path.

Before starting Silverview Credit Partners, my current company, I spent more than six years working for UBS. The bulk of my experience started with the 2008 financial crisis when the Swiss-based, multinational company brought me in to head up a team, focused on cleaning up their distressed investments. 2008 was a difficult year in the world of finance, but I looked at the opportunity I had been given to create solutions as an exciting one. I managed a global team, handling over forty billion dollars worth of assets, and the result was some of the most interesting work of my career.

Working for a large company like UBS, I was very fortunate to receive numerous opportunities. I was not just on board to direct their dynamic, financial portfolios. I was leading people, and that afforded me the opportunity to learn from a variety of different management styles. The company highly valued its employees, treating them like assets, and they spared no expense in supporting its managers with top-end strategies.

The situation with my current company is different. We are much smaller. Our entire staff is smaller than just one of the teams I used to manage for UBS. It was during a seminar I took while running Silverview Credit Partners, where I first became interested in Chris Voss, and discovered his principles of empathic leadership.

Something I discovered is that workplace culture is critically important, regardless of the size of your company or team. How you inform and develop that culture ends up being quite different. When you're running a small business, largely guiding your own ship, there isn't the same institutional pressure coming down from the Human Resources department. No one is asking you to enroll in a leadership seminar. Running a smaller company, you have to be intentional, meaning, if you want to develop those skills, you have to take that initiative for yourself.

Among the most impactful seminars I took through UBS taught me something called SCARF, written about by David Rock. This specific style of leadership taught me how to get in better touch with people's needs. Even today, years later, I still use these techniques in my interactions.

SCARF is invaluable because it helps target strategies for identifying a person's core motivation. Workplace leaders are responsible for giving their employees the company's core vision and the guidance necessary for successfully meeting that mission. But at the same time, we also need to recognize that they are human beings, each one with basic needs. When a leader is able to identify and understand what those needs are, and especially how to motivate them, the result is a more successful employee.

SCARF is an acronym where each letter stands for a different motivating attribute. The idea is that while every single one of us possesses each one of these attributes in some way, each person prioritizes them differently. They essentially create their own hierarchy.

These motivating attributes are:

- Status – identifies employee or persons who are driven by labels and positions.
- Certainty – acknowledges the need some people have to receive consistency in their environment without the threat of volatility.
- Autonomy – is for the kind of people that thrive on functioning alone.
- Relatedness – is for those that need their space to be part of a connected environment.
- Fairness – allows us to honor people or employees who strive for equality.

It's a lot to digest, but if you take just a moment to look at each of these attributes, it's hard not to start identifying which attributes are most important to yourself.

Even an ideal workplace cannot be all things to all people. But when we, as leaders, take the necessary time required to recognize what motivates our people and respond to their core needs accordingly, we move closer to maximizing worker output. Instead of forcing one-size-fits-all policies, we are able to meet someone where they are and help guide them to where they want themselves to go.

At Silverview, culture is important to us. We take ownership of our leadership style and, as a result, we're able to positively affect our work culture from top to bottom.

FINDING A NICHE IN THE MIDDLE

The 2008 financial crisis created a great deal of hardship for many American households. Reverberations resulting from that disaster can still be felt today in how our economy functions. For my company, Silverview Credit Partners, however, the uncertainty in our teetering financial system opened the door for a rare and exciting opportunity.

It also leads to a fundamental tenet of empathic leadership: if you are able to identify someone's problem, you can help them create a solution.

Post-financial crisis, regulators manifested a fundamental shift in the American lending space. In essence, changes were proposed to safeguard the economy from ever having to endure such a precarious stress test again, but when those changing regulations went into place, they created something interesting: a doughnut hole in available financing. Borrowers looking for smaller business loans, in the range of one to five million dollars, had plenty of options; the same was true for borrowers seeking larger loans, thirty million dollars and up. If you were a business in any industry looking for financing in the range between five and thirty, you were out of luck. There was nowhere for you to go.

This problem in the lending markets allowed a willing upstart a clear niche. Seeing the solution to that problem as an opportunity, Silverview Credit Partners was born.

Going out on my own, I had a great deal of support from UBS, my previous company. It was quite a welcome feeling to launch into a new business with the knowledge that, if things didn't go quite right, we would have an option to fall back on.

But I believed in the vision we launched. My team spends a lot of time going out, looking at prospective borrowers. We travel around the country, and the world, visiting innovators and meeting with creators. I often find myself marveling at the sheer creativity and innovation that supports our economy.

Technology affords us the opportunity to take in a lot of meetings, allowing us to operate on a truly global level. However, real and lasting connections, I believe, come face to face. I love sitting down with someone and learning their vision for new and amazing businesses. Even more than that, I am fascinated by the many interesting people working to get them off of the ground.

My company has, over the last few years, seen a number of sales of legacy businesses. In these increasingly common scenarios, the owners of medium to large family-run companies are reaching retirement age – in some cases, pushed beyond because of COVID – and want to move on with the knowledge that what they have spent their lives building will continue on in their stead.

The nature of business is changing, though. Sometimes, when left without a natural heir in the immediate family to pass the operation on to take over, those baby boomer-spawned businesses are being forced to go up for sale. Looking at our niche, funding medium-sized loans, we've been able to loan the capital necessary to facilitate those transfers, keeping brands and businesses alive.

Every month, Silverview Credit Partners reviews somewhere in the range of one hundred and fifty to two hundred transactions. On the surface, our business is about lending money. While that might be our core function, what it really comes down to more is about building relationships. We thrive on effective communication, built on active listening, and gaining an understanding of the people with whom we want to work.

A WORK CULTURE FOR THE FUTURE

Since starting Silverview Credit Partners, we have successfully found a niche in the global financial lending market to flourish in. But that is not the only thing that defines who we are.

In the beginning, the COVID-19-influenced decision to take the company completely remote was a tough one on me. Ultimately, however, it has proven to be a successful move. Our culture has not suffered. In fact, I think we've thrived.

Much of our work, as is dictated by its global nature, is held in virtual space but we still prioritize meeting the people we work with in person. There are absolutely critical things that you can only learn about a person when you sit across the table from them. Zoom is great, without this tool, it would have been impossible to operate a business during COVID, but it doesn't replace the human connection.

Our team meets once a week in a virtual space. We take that time to get the chance to check in with one another and connect. Then on a quarterly basis, we gather in person for team-building activities. We've volunteered at food banks. Last year we volunteered in Dallas for Build-A-Bike where we assembled bicycles for disadvantaged children.

Silverview Credit Partners may be relatively small in comparison to other larger companies. However, I stand behind the work culture we have established; we are outstanding, not just in what we do, but the people we do it with. When everyone went remote in response to COVID-19 in 2020, my fear was that a healthy, nurturing workplace culture would disappear for those that needed it. Thankfully, I was wrong.

The American workforce has endured its share of profound challenges over the last twenty years. There will be, no doubt, more challenges coming in the future. Whether SCARF is the strategy, or something similar is adopted, tactical empathy stands as the centerpiece for creating a culture that is not only something we are proud to stand behind but will provide the kind of responsive environment that allows our staff to thrive.

About Adam

Adam Hagfors is the Managing Partner and Chief Investment Officer of Silverview Credit Partners. Silverview specializes in debt solutions to businesses and individuals who seek $10mm to $30mm in capital.

Prior to founding Silverview Credit Partners in 2015, Adam was the Global Head of the Legacy Group and America's Head of the Non-Core and Legacy Group at UBS AG, where he managed a global team spanning a variety of fixed income asset classes across a $40 billion portfolio. During this time, he served on the UBS Group Americas Executive Committee, the UBS Group Americas Risk and Control Committee, and the UBS Investment Bank Americas Risk Committee. Adam had been with UBS from 2009-2015. Previously, he worked at JP Morgan and Bear Stearns, focused on structured credit and corporate credit products.

Throughout his career, Adam has participated in numerous corporate boards and speaking engagements.

Adam is also actively involved in his community, serving as Treasurer for the Frederica Academy Board of Trustees and a member of the St Bart's Community Preschool Advisory Board. Previously, Adam was the Co-Chair of the St Bart's Community Preschool Advisory Board and a member of The Browning School's Board of Trustees.

He earned his B.S. in Business Administration and Accounting at Washington and Lee University.

Adam and his wife Jenn reside on St. Simons Island, GA with their two sons, Andersen and Jensen.

You can learn more about Adam and Silverview Credit at:

- www.silverview.com

CHAPTER 10

WE ARE WHO WE ARE EVERY DAY

BY JANET VONKOHN

FAMILY LEADERSHIP

It was January of 2017 when my twenty-three year old, college educated, independent daughter came to visit my husband and me. She was traveling in from another state because she wanted to take part in planning our twenty-fifth wedding anniversary party. We were both honored and charmed to spend the afternoon reminiscing and watching the videos from our wedding day.

The day started out being such fun. We reconnected and laughed while taking a couple of hours walking down memory lane.

Later, I joined my husband in the living room. I remember our daughter came in and sat alone on the coffee table facing both of us. Then she cleared her throat and took a very serious tone. Unbeknownst to either of us, our lives and relationship were about to take a drastic turn.

"I have something to tell you," she said.

I looked at my husband, spellbound with curiosity. What did she want to talk about? We hadn't bargained for any surprises.

"I'm pregnant."

I was stunned and speechless. My daughter had been dating the same young man for about a year and their relationship had recently ended. At that point in time, we had met her boyfriend twice and what stuck with her father and I was how mentally, emotionally, and physically upset she was by their most recent break-up. She had not been in a good place for some time.

As dumbfounded as I was, my husband, her father, stepped up. He responded to her revelation by showing an abundance of empathetic leadership. Everything in his actions demonstrated the kind of love that a father has for his daughter. I remember that he stood up from his chair, wrapped his arms around her, held her, and hugged her tightly. They both cried like babies.

"I'm sorry, I'm sorry," she kept on muttering into his chest.

"It's OK, it's OK," my husband replied.

Looking back, I can say, I have never experienced anything more loving and beautiful than the moment they shared. My husband was the quintessential empathetic leader for our family.

What about me? How did I respond?

In hindsight, I screwed up. I said everything wrong and that came at a huge cost to our relationship. If I could go back and hit the rewind button, I would have responded exactly like her father, feeling certain that we would not have experienced the relational valley that we traveled for the next eighteen months.

AN OVERNIGHT SUCCESS WAS TEN YEARS IN THE MAKING

Hard work is a part of who I am. Giving my all to the important things in my life, whether that be business or family, is like second nature to me. In college, I studied biology and chemistry. I enrolled with the intention of graduating and going on to med school and becoming a medical doctor.

Coming from a lower income military family, I had to work my way through school. Coupled with parental help, student loans, and Pell grants, I typically held down two or three jobs simultaneously to make enough money to keep up with my educational expenses. Nothing in my life had ever been handed to me, so hard work was my norm.

One of my jobs was working for a local medical supply company. We were selling medical disposables used for physical therapy patients. Each evening from around five until nine, I would come into the office and make outbound calls. These were cold calls, meaning I had nothing more than a name and a number but using a no pressure, conversational sales technique, I sold more than anyone else on the team.

When it came to converting, I was a natural.

I remember that I graduated from college on a Saturday. The company I had been doing sales for made me a job offer, starting the following Monday. It seemed like a pretty good opportunity. At the very least, it was something I already knew I was good at, so I accepted. Before I knew it, my dream of going into med school was in the rearview, and I was working in medical supply sales full time.

Even though I continued to be good at sales, as a full-time job, I just didn't like it. It didn't take long for me to realize that it was not for me. I consulted with a local recruiting company with the hopes of changing positions, and they sent me out on an interview to a pharmaceutical company.

While I didn't end up getting the job they set me up with, curiously enough, the recruiting firm surprised me with an offer of a position. I could see right away that this change would be a good move for me. From my first taste of the recruiting world, I loved it and I would have stayed with the company forever, climbing their ladder, but about a year after starting, I moved to another state. Knowing that I was forced to change jobs, the move presented me with an unexpected opportunity.

Maybe I could start my own recruiting company?

I had never set out to become an entrepreneur. Like so many businesspeople before me, the call that I answered was highly unexpected. Sometimes youth and inexperience can be beneficial.

I started my own recruiting company in the mid-1980's. The little start-up company that became the VonKohn Search Group didn't have much, but back then, there wasn't much you really needed to get going. Getting a recruiting company off the ground came with a low barrier to entry.

I had an office and a desk. I kept a day planner for appointments and a rolodex where I managed my growing list of phone contacts. When we started out, I remember that we had to run out and mail paper resumes through the local post office. When I finally got my first fax machine, it could only transmit five pages at a time.

"Why would I ever need to send more than five pages?" I remember thinking to myself.

Nearly thirty-eight years later, my office looks much different. While on the surface, a lot in business has evolved with the times. In other ways, things are exactly the same now as when I made my first cold call.

Recruiting was then, as it is now, a people-centric business. Successful placements are built through establishing and maintaining meaningful connections. Always remember, your network is your net worth, and it behooves you to build long-term relationships. By reaching out and cold calling and building rapport, which I did a lot of, using my old landline phone with the spiral cord, I slowly built the foundational relationships necessary for success.

As many meaningful connections a businessperson makes, an equal number of people end up hanging up on you. Without a track record or a reputation, you're just another company looking for an angle into a competitive market. I had that inner unrelenting drive to succeed though. In those early days, I was in my mid-twenties, filled with grit and determination. I was going to succeed at any cost. I wanted success as badly as I wanted air. I grew up as a military brat from a lower income family and was absolutely determined not to wear hand-me-down clothes anymore.

I often worked seven days a week when I started. There were absolutely no boundaries. After maybe fifteen years, I gradually cut my workload back to six days. It took me more than twenty years to pull that back to five, allowing myself a conventional weekend.

This is why I am fond of saying, I'm an overnight success that took ten years. Success is like a snowball. Once it gets rolling, it grows exponentially, and that has been my experience through the decades.

EMPATHY AS THE ENGINE FOR A PEOPLE BUSINESS

I come from the core personal belief that how you do anything is how you do everything. Empathetic leadership applies equally throughout a company, from the top corporate position, CEO and heads of companies, on down – the same way that it extends to marriages, families, friendships, colleagues and even classmates.

We can all be leaders without necessarily needing to wear that leader title.

I got into the recruiting business because I discovered I had a knack for working with people. Many years later, no matter how much technology has changed the tactics of how I perform the tasks involved in my day-to-day work, it remains, at its heart, a people business.

Our basic function is to place people in a new job. How that placement goes has a tremendous impact on the quality of their lives, from the trajectory of their careers and families to their financial livelihood. On the flip side, we get the opportunity to work directly with the heads of hiring for major companies. These are driven, career-minded people, and we relish the opportunity to help them meet their corporate goals and visions.

People place a great deal of emotion in their work. When we place someone in a new position, we get to celebrate their big win with them. These are some of our favorite moments. When someone we previously placed loses their job, an unfortunate reality of any economy, forcing them back onto the market, we are there to help them pick up the pieces.

No one likes getting let go. Unpleasant questions tend to come up.

What am I going to do without a paycheck? How am I going to feed my kids? The world often seems like it's ending. However, it is our job to turn things around, becoming the engine that helps them start over.

Those person-to-person fundamentals are the same. I employed the same empathic listening and communication skills when I started as I do today.

Operating a successful recruiting business relies on a few core principles. At the very top of those is building and maintaining strong interpersonal relationships. On any given day, I need to be able to convince a Fortune 500 company that I can find their next executive level employee as well as earn the trust of that ambitious worker looking to make a leap into a new position.

How do I manage that tightrope? I rely on a healthy dose of empathy.

In my experience, people are more alike than they are different. Everyone shares the desire to be heard and feel like their needs are valued. When I take the time to listen to that prospective employee, I hear that they want equitable treatment from their employers and good relationships with their co-workers. They want fair compensation for the work they're doing.

What does empathy look like in day-to-day practice?

Whoever I'm working with, I spend the necessary time early on to get to know who they are. What matters to them. What's important? I want to deeply understand what they are looking for in a new job, especially when it comes to their salary, responsibilities, and travel, among other factors.

Listening gives me information. That information I can use to make a smarter placement. When an open position that I am recruiting for is not a match, I don't bother to connect them to my client. What would be the point? If travel is a deal breaker for someone then there is no reason to send them on an interview for a job that requires half time travel. In a similar way of thinking, if that person's expectations don't match their experience, I tell them. It can be difficult for someone to hear, but honesty builds trust, and trust is the starting point for those foundational relationships.

Listening empathically also allows me to address the growing importance of social issues within the modern workplace. The subject of diversity, while still relatively new, requires an empathic approach. Prospective employees self-identify in ways that might seem different, or counterintuitive to an older generation, unaccustomed to accommodating such wishes. I myself have been caught misidentifying someone's gender, much to my embarrassment.

What do I do in an instance like this? I listen to what the person wants and adjust my behavior accordingly. Providing an empathic environment isn't about me. It's about the people I work with everyday feeling respected and heard.

THE FUTURE

My daughter has grown into such a wonderful woman. Among her many amazing qualities is her enormous capacity for forgiveness – even in the most trying situations.

On the day she revealed her pregnancy, I did everything wrong. All that I could think about was myself. I was disappointed and angry. I was scared for her. I kept asking the question, how was she going to take care of the child?

Everything about my reaction was about how her news affected me. Unfortunately, nothing in my response had anything to do with her. I remember feeling embarrassed about her situation. Looking back on my behavior now, I'm disappointed that I didn't know how to respond better.

I am grateful that her father, my husband, displayed the perfect example of empathetic family leadership in that very sensitive moment. I am also grateful that our family has a lot of love built up over the years in our "love tank", otherwise that behavior had the potential to negatively affect our relationship for years to come. The good news is, we have since worked through it. My daughter is married with a beautiful daughter of her own to love. Just as I have learned from her, she is now in the season of learning from her daughter.

The future of my business, on the surface, continues to evolve and change with the times. Workers have become more transient. They change jobs more often now than ever before and that challenge is not likely to go away. We face periodic economic uncertainties, like we did in 2008 and 2020, which forces us into the hopeful role of steadying an uncertain workforce.

Currently, I hear a lot of concerns about the tremendous uncertainties posed by artificial intelligence. But at the risk of sounding naive, I remain optimistic.

Why do I feel good about the future?

Because people will always need people. The quality of your life directly correlates to the quality of your relationships. And always be mindful that a little empathy goes a long way.

About Janet

As Founder and CEO / President of VonKohn Search Group, Janet VonKohn along with her team, partners with National Life Science Companies to build world-class Commercial, Clinical, and Executive Teams.

VSG is nationally recognized and awarded as a driving, results-oriented, self-starting team of professional recruiters whose sense of urgency is tempered and disciplined by their concern for the accuracy and quality of work. VSG has helped companies create winning teams for over 30 years. Through a personal and relentless process, they partner with their clients' leadership team to hire and retain elite talent. By creating customized talent pipelines, VSG keeps their clients ahead of the curve.

Janet's experience includes overseeing hundreds of clients each year. She personally trains leadership on how to recruit, hire, and retain the best talent. She teaches specific hiring / interviewing strategies along with proven employee retention methods. Janet also provides consulting services to C-level executives that find themselves in a career transition or need confidential guidance in their current role.

Janet became a serial entrepreneur in 1987 when she started her first company, Professional Search Consultants, a Florida-based recruiting firm. Since that time, she co-founded National Sales Network, a national search firm focused on building sales teams for the pharmaceutical industry. She has been an angel investor in multiple biopharmaceutical start-ups including Clene Nanomedicine and others. She is an investor and Strategic Advisor for Ennaid Therapeutics, a pre-commercial pharmaceutical company that focuses on rare diseases in underserved populations of the world. Finally, she is a partner in NashVirgin, LLC which is a growing commercial real estate business with properties in multiple states.

Her Superpowers are simplifying complex issues, creating common visions, and unifying teams to exceed goals.

Janet has been married to her husband, Lon, since Valentine's Day 1992, and together they have two grown children and one grand princess. Their grown children have followed the family's entrepreneurial mindset with one leading projects for VSG and the other in the Music Business. Janet and Lon enjoy traveling the world, immersing themselves in other cultures, keeping healthy and fit, intentionally creating memories with family and friends, but mostly spending time enjoying each other.

For more information, please visit:

- www.vonkohnsearchgroup.com
- https://www.linkedin.com/in/janetblumenvonkohn/

CHAPTER 11

"PIZZA, MOVIES, AND REAL ESTATE!"

BY MIKEL DUSI

THERE'S NO ALGORITHM FOR EXPERIENCE: WORK WORKS!

To succeed in life, grab every opportunity with unwavering and genuine enthusiasm. Commit to taking massive, calculated, and direct actionable steps on a clearly defined roadmap.

While life can be bumpy, each bump is a test; a test of fortitude and commitment to living a life on purpose, not by accident. Give yourself a chance and venture into the business jungle—and make sure to double, triple, or quadruple your failure rate. Failure is a part of life. It is how we advance and grow from these mistakes that defines us. Learned mistakes in any discipline forge an expert.

I was first introduced to customer service at my parents' pizzeria in Ozone Park, Queens, NY during the 1990's. There, I encountered a diverse cast of customers—or 'characters'—as I like to call them. These interactions were the foundation of my unique communication style, providing a space where I learned to deal with difficult people and situations. As I matured, this proved invaluable in managing my parents' real estate businesses.

The foundation of successful relationships rests in the power of dynamic silence and the art of active listening. If you want to be *interesting*, then you must be *interested* in their story. The more personal, the more powerful. To capture interest, show genuine curiosity. *Listening to respond* versus *listening to understand* are two entirely different things. Engaging in another's story, seeking ways to assist rather than waiting for your turn to speak, lays the foundation for authentic trust.

Navigating life with the comforts I had in New York was too easy. I never planned or even dreamt of leaving NY. I had a life that was already too good to be true. However, the call for adventure proved too irresistible for this Queens kid! Hollywood was the ticket, and I decided to take the leap. My time there was a rollercoaster of growth; I discovered how to hustle harder, faster, smarter, and more economically than most.

I was not content mingling with just anyone in the industry. I wanted to be around the big guns, the real decision-makers. I positioned myself to get in front of heavy hitting deal makers, the seasoned film producers who navigated the business jungles and came out victorious. I once asked an accomplished producer for advice on where to dive into the industry. He said, "Embrace it all! Stick to feature films over TV. You're young! Take this as your grand adventure. Travel, learn, and leave your mark!" It was like the beginning of an epic journey. Most people settle into one niche, but I jumped into every department. Nothing was off limits to me. Under the mentorship of two veteran film producers, I dove insanely deep into learning all aspects of film. These producers gave me all the keys to their kingdom. Given their Jewish heritage, they held a deep loyalty to family, friends, and community. They recognized that same loyalty in me, a Kosovar Albanian kid from Queens.

Moreover, they didn't just value me as an asset; they embraced me as family. They became my California kin, standing by me through all ups and downs. They shared with me lessons, experiences, and wisdom from screenplay development and directorial insights, to casting bankable actors for domestic and international financing. I was immersed in the global film distribution scene, frequenting renowned festivals from Sundance and Cannes to Toronto and Venice. It started with development, followed by pre-production, then physical production. After that came post-production, leading to distribution—from theatrical releases to video on demand.

Film school wasn't part of my journey. Instead, it was work school! My knack became listening to what departments needed and staying resourceful enough to keep our team on budget and on time. I consistently found ways to add value to the production, but one duty always stood out: airport pickups. I earned enough trust with my mentors to greet the incoming talent, studio heads, and financiers. I loved to make sure we always made a great first impression of our production. This task, overlooked by many as unproductive, afforded me rare access to production's MVPs. The proximity to them and their invaluable lessons far surpassed traditional education. Ensuring satisfaction was important—as you never get a second chance to make a great first impression.

No task was beneath me. From checking on the MVPs' families in their origin cities while they were on set with us to canceling the lead actress' boyfriend's acting role and flight because she had begun an on-set relationship with the lead actor, my responsibilities were vast and unpredictable. No matter the situation, I made it a point to provide people with what I now recognize as 'accusation audits'— clear, advanced warnings about myself and the production. This way, none of these power players could claim ignorance about what they were stepping into.

When the entire cast and crew are all flown in and settled, it is standard practice to call a production meeting. This is where you set the tone. It became typical for me to tell various department heads, "Stay on budget, I'll have to say 'no' to additional departmental expenses, and it might not be pleasant hearing it. So, I apologize in advance." Over time, I learned how important it was to communicate important details to department heads. For instance, "We're going into night shoots next week. Come 3 AM, fatigue will hit, and your bones will ache. Rest up during the day to make the nights easier." Or a simple location note: "You might not be thrilled with the drive to the shooting location since it's quite a distance from the hotel. However, it's a unique location that we're very fortunate to have and that will look incredible on camera." This boosts morale for a crew that is about to jump on a van staying a distance away from a non-accessible location.

I like to say, "It's important to be on the exact same page in terms of what's happening and what to expect. I'm not going to tell you. Instead,

I'm going to show you with my actions that we have each other's backs on this set. By the end of this journey, we won't just be an unstoppable team; we'll be family," to unify the team.

BE AGGRESSIVELY PATIENT

There came a pivotal moment when I realized it was time for a new chapter in my life. This realization was largely influenced by my relationship with the most extraordinary woman I have ever met—the woman who would become my wife and the mother of my children. From our very first encounter, I knew she was a once-in-a-lifetime kind of person. I felt an undeniable connection and instantly expressed how special she was—a sentiment that proved true in every sense of the word. The film industry, especially when you're thriving, can be a whirlwind. One minute you're on set in one country, and the next, you're off to another for a film premiere. It's a life of constant transitions. In the early days of our relationship, my then-future wife pointed out a hard truth: I was not present, particularly with her. I wasn't truly listening. That feedback was a wake-up call, pushing me to dig deeper and truly understand her needs and desires.

I started to listen. I recognized the essence of her happiness, which, in turn, would be my happiness. However, I soon realized that my constant absences due to film commitments wouldn't sustain our relationship. It became clear I needed a healthy pivot.

Given my background, my expertise boiled down to three things: pizza, movies, and real estate. While I love pizza, I was more interested in making the dough, pun absolutely intended, than the actual pie. With everything laid out, the path became clear. I embarked on my next journey of buying and selling properties.

THERE'S NO GOOD IN ANYTHING
UNTIL IT'S FINISHED

Real estate shares similarities with the movie industry. Both require quick thinking, creativity, and the ability to identify and address pain points. Success in these fields hinges on knowledge, resources, respect, and preparation to take direct action.

Proposals from billion dollar iBuyers and premiere local realtors often find their way onto the living room tables of prospective sellers. It suits me to find out if I am 'THE FAVORITE OR THE FOOL'—a real prospect or just another suspect. This requires me to utilize an accusation audit over here, a proof of life question over there, and see what sticks. The more questions answered, the better we are able to service their needs.

Observing other proposals on a seller's table, I often ask, "I know you're discussing offers with other people, so why am I here?" Their response helps me tailor my approach to address what others might be missing. Sellers tell me, "I don't want to pay commissions!" or "I don't want to do any repairs!" or "I want the buyer to cover all closing costs!" and most frequently, "I want you to pay me in an all-cash offer." Many are simply looking for someone with a hands-on, proven history to stop an impending foreclosure in its tracks. With this feedback, I can pinpoint what's missing and help them more than other buyers. If challenges arise at the closing stage, I revisit the seller's priorities to ensure a smooth conclusion.

I learned the power of never asking clients to *sign* anything. Instead, I ask them to *approve, authorize,* or *endorse*. For a little fun, I request their *autograph*. Rather than using the term *contract*, which can be intimidating, I always shoot for soft words like *paperwork* or *understanding*. For instance, I say, "I have a simple 3-page agreement summarizing everything. If you could *approve* here, *authorize* there, and let me get your *autograph*, that'd be perfect!"

'Accusation audits,' or as others like to call them, 'the usual suspects,' are indispensable. These include, "You might assume that I'm just like every other buyer and that I'm only here to give you a lowball price." And specifically in my case, "You might think I'm just a fast-talking New Yorker with boundless energy who is just here to sell you the Queensborough Bridge; however, by the end of our meeting, you'll have a clearer understanding of the best direction for you and your property."

In the film industry, each project presents its own unique set of challenges. Similarly, in real estate, each property has its own unique challenges as well.

My team handles a range of situations, from foreclosures and short sales, to options and master lease options. We can buy directly at wholesale or connect sellers with our buyers' list using a retail-oriented approach. My real estate mentor equipped me with every tool for success: books, audio cassettes, conferences, and seminars. Above all, it was his hands-on guidance that mattered most. He connected me with his own powerhouse mentor, which became an immediate, life-changing experience! My mentor schooled me in the art of asking pointed questions that yield incredible results, much like Chris Voss's calibrated questions. Each question has a distinct and purposeful aim.

My expertise as an investor lies in flipping homes and multi-unit properties, such as apartment complexes. I also have a knack for identifying and acquiring distressed properties—those in foreclosure or disrepair. Leads come from sellers grappling with challenging life circumstances—be it a family death, enduring illness, divorce, or job relocation. Given their vulnerable states, these individuals need to trust me. It's unfortunate but true that many out there look to exploit these sellers, capitalizing on their lack of awareness about available options. I take pride in ensuring these sellers are well-informed about every potential avenue—be it refinancing, securing hard money loans from institutions or private parties, making property repairs to boost appeal, or selling as a short sale or at retail. For many of these sellers, we are discussing their single most valuable asset—their home—and I'm committed to helping them navigate their predicament.

Assisting people in difficult circumstances demands understanding their needs and a specialized approach tailored to each unique situation. Instead of boasting about accomplishments, my primary focus is providing them a roadmap with real, actionable solutions. For instance, if a homeowner is on the brink of foreclosure, their main concern is preventing the bank from stealing their home. I emphasize and craft a custom, clear, step-by-step plan with a distinct beginning, middle, and end. I offer a range of solutions to save their home from foreclosure, often incorporating strategies that allow them to remain in their homes. Demonstrating a clear vision and a proven track record speaks volumes more than any self-praise or company accolades. This principle is reminiscent of Chris's experience in the Haitian hostage scenario.

SHOW ME YOUR MENTORS, AND I'LL SHOW YOU YOUR FUTURE

You don't just need any mentor – you need the right mentor. The most invaluable lessons in my life came from the adult figures who shaped my childhood years. My karate sensei and high school football coaches represent two of these powerhouse figures. My sensei was more than just a martial arts trainer; he ingrained in me the kind of discipline that life demands. My high school football coaches, on the other hand, taught me about accountability, responsibility, and team development.

Other mentors include the film producers who broadened my cinematic horizons and real estate mentors who guided me through property intricacies. Each has played a pivotal role in shaping my journey. However, there are two mentors whose mark trumps all: my parents.

My father's mentorship and the challenging lessons we faced together stand out. While I hold my mother, family, and friends close, my father occupies a unique and unmatched space in my life. He is my true north star, my personal hero, and I am his biggest fan! Whether it was observing him at our pizzerias or managing real estate properties, he pushed forward with relentless vigor, never once complaining. He is the living, breathing personification of endurance and passion for life.

I witnessed my father and mother accomplish remarkable successes in life. Above all, it was the passion and drive of both my parents that lit a fire in me, one that continues to blaze. Those invaluable days spent working alongside family in the restaurant were more than just moments; they were foundational lessons that laid the groundwork for my success today. The rigorous work, the learning opportunities, and the time with them are experiences I am deeply grateful for. These life experiences were the greatest gifts a son could ever ask for. Gifts whose value I can only hope to instill in my children and all of you reading this today.

"When all is said and done... you gotta put in the work!"

About Mikel

Mikel Dusi brings a wealth of expertise to the *"Empathetic Leadership"* project. His background involves team centralism, multi-million-dollar negotiations, agile mitigation, and the art of implementing growth multipliers that secure performance-based results. Mikel is passionate about being a liaison between vision and success. His career spans over 20 years of experience advancing pipeline efficiencies and overall organizational success in multiple industries.

Born and raised in New York and of Kosovar Albanian descent, Mike recalls his early days as a pizza boy for his family's pizzeria in Ozone Park, Queens. In 2003, he made a significant change by trading the cityscapes of New York for the sunny vibes of California. Not long after, Mikel's professional journey hit the ground running as a testament to his diverse skill set and upbringings.

Mikel began his career in the film industry, where he led various productions and managed logistics for feature films, short films, pilots, commercials, and music videos. During this time, Mikel accelerated production objectives and fundamentally interlaced system-level thinking. His expertise spans domestic and international development, finance, pre-production, physical production, and post-production, as well as distribution scaling theatrical to digital. His dedication to raising creative standards and industry galvanizations earned him immense respect among his peers.

Beyond his illustrious film career, Mikel carved a niche as a distinguished real estate investor. He excels in revitalizing distressed multi-unit properties and single-family homes. His hallmark of transparent communication, adept relationship-building, and commitment to mutually beneficial transactions cultivated a strong investment portfolio and a trusted clientele. Mikel attributes his versatile professional journey to his laser-beam focused skill-set of active listening and negotiation.

Mikel believes in creating better business and community futures by instilling positive impacts. Mikel is an elite keynote conversationalist, distinguished TEDx guest speaker, televised interviewee, and a globally recognized presenter. He keeps a firm pulse on industry evolutions and introductions, demonstrated through his active participation in various Hollywood, real estate, and technology functions.

Mikel Dusi's involvement in *Empathetic Leadership* provides a distinctive viewpoint on leadership, innovation, and achieving organizational success, making it an asset for individuals aspiring to lead with both empathy and foresight.

Still a New Yorker at heart, he is happy to be soaking up the Los Angeles sun and embracing the Cali lifestyle. And, while Mikel is passionate about helping people turn their dreams into reality, he finds his greatest joy in every moment he gets to spend with his wife and children.

CHAPTER 12

ONE CLICK—HOW YOU CAN LOSE YOUR BUSINESS IN A SECOND

BY BARBARA PALUSZKIEWICZ

The owner of a small family-run business clicked his mouse. The action took less than a second, but the result was a loss of over $4 million.

Here's how it happened:

The controller at the company received an email saying one of their vendors had changed their bank account information. The controller forwarded it to the owner, who was in a hurry at the time. He didn't take the time to double-check its legitimacy, and he updated the banking information. Unbeknownst to them, they paid the wrong supplier for three months.

That accounted for $2 million being transferred to the cybercriminals. Another $2 million had to be paid to the correct supplier as they were in arrears and needed to meet the contractual commitments to their customers. That's to say nothing of the legal fees to determine who was at fault since insurance covered none of it.

Many business owners don't realize how vulnerable they are when it comes to IT matters, and they don't fully appreciate that everything can collapse…with just one click.

As the CEO of CDN Technologies, which is an IT service and IT support company (aka – a Managed Service Provider, or MSP), I have the responsibility to fix their technical problems *and* show them empathy for what they're going through. Demonstrating understanding is the only way we can work together to turn the situation around.

After an attack or a scam, many people are paralyzingly afraid of the technology, and that has a serious and detrimental effect on their business moving forward. A large part of my job is calming people down enough to realize a mistake was made, we fixed it, we set it up so it can't happen again, and it's time to put it behind them.

Apart from fixing the issue and preventing another one, I need to 'click' that part of my client's brain that gets them to say, "You know what? I'm going to leave this to IT."

MY PATH TO IT

Being in IT was very much a fluke. I originally went to university for chemistry and physics, hoping to get a job in the pharmaceutical space. When I was given my offer letter to a major pharmaceutical company, I was thrilled. It felt like the culmination of all my hard work. Then two of their main products were pulled from the shelves, and suddenly the company had a hiring freeze. Shortly after, my offer letter was rescinded.

Always interested in technology, I was intrigued when an opportunity presented itself shortly after to be a founding partner in a new company, CDN Technologies. Within the technology market, I saw a significant piece missing. People would come in and very matter-of-factly address IT issues. They often didn't take into consideration how stressful the situation was for the business owners or individuals. With CDN, I had the opportunity to bring empathy into the equation.

As soon as I started, everything clicked. I loved the work, and I knew IT was my calling. Customers appreciated the technical skills I brought to the table, but they were even more grateful for the empathy I showed them and the understanding I demonstrated about how difficult and stressful these IT issues can be.

For the next twenty years, my team and I grew the company. Today, I'm the founder and CEO of a highly rated, accredited company providing IT solutions and services across Canada. After accidentally falling into the industry several decades ago, I've since gained recognition and expertise in the IT security space. I wrote a book *IT Scams: How to Avoid Being Ripped Off* and have spoken everywhere from podcasts to television to Carnegie Hall.

However, through all of my accomplishments, I know any success I've had has hinged on one thing – genuine empathy.

THE GREATEST MISCONCEPTION ABOUT IT

When people think about IT, they think about technology. Software. Devices. Systems. They forget there's always a human on the other side of that screen. IT is all about dealing with people, and you always have to be sensitive to their feelings and the real-world ramifications of their technological issues.

Having sustained success in the technology sphere requires a great deal of empathy. When people experience a problem with their IT, they're usually scared. Or angry. Or nervous. Our job at that point is twofold. Having the knowledge and technical skill sets to address, fix, or mitigate the issue and being empathetic to their situation. In order to help, we must actively listen to what they're saying and understand what they're going through. If we don't do that, we can't hope to take them from that negative space to a positive experience.

Being able to understand someone else's feelings is the most important professional lesson I've ever learned. Being sensitive to another person's emotional state—and respecting it—has been the key to CDN's continued success. Even in a landscape dominated by firewalls and malware, we never forget our industry is fundamentally human. People run these systems. People are affected when things go wrong.

When we offer preventative training, we're helping real people be more secure with their data, companies, and money.

MAKING EMPATHY A FOUNDATION OF CDN TECHNOLOGIES

Every employee at our company has to go through extensive customer service training. This ensures they know how to speak to people—even when they come to us during incredibly stressful situations. (Bank fraud. Rogue employees. Ransomware. Compromised emails.) Even when millions are on the line, we have to be that calming presence in the room.

Our people are experts on technical issues, and we also prioritize those soft skills. At the end of the day, we know empathy in the technical space is a skill that can be taught and improved upon, and we do it by learning from the best training material available. This training helps incredibly smart engineers and technicians understand and frame the human side of every problem.

In IT, there's a lot of technical jargon. When there's a security problem, it's equally important our employees understand two things. All the technical know-how to fix the issue and the human-to-human language to convey to customers what's happening, what safety measures are being implemented, and why.

In this way, our employees are a lot like first responders. They're dealing with alarming, stressful, serious problems, but they need tact and genuine empathy to provide the help and guidance necessary to get to the other side.

WHY EMPATHY MATTERS EVEN MORE WITH CYBERCRIME

While many forget about the role of empathy in IT security, it's arguably even more important in these scenarios. Why?

- **Victims Don't Get Sympathy**

Victims of most other crimes get sympathy, but when you're the victim of a cyberattack, you're often labeled as irresponsible or careless. An IT provider needs to come to the situation with all the empathy and support you'd bring to any other crime victim.

The customer needs to know you're going to work together to figure this out.

- **Cybercrime Can Happen Fast**

During presentations, I have people hold up their index finger and click in the air. I remind them that's how long it takes to fall victim to one of these scams and to lose everything.

- **Schemes Today Are Incredibly Sophisticated**

When a client's Facebook account was hacked, he didn't think much of it. He figured it was the kind of benign cyber-activity that happened all the time. What he forgot was that some of his work passwords were the same as his Facebook password. The threat actor (the 'bad guy') viewed his LinkedIn profile, capitalized on the wealth of information exposed on that profile, and logged into the cloud portal of his company's payroll software.

Once the threat actor had access to payroll, he simply added himself as a company employee, and he drew a paycheck for the next *six months.* When Christmas rolled around, he wrote himself a sizable bonus check, and that was the red flag that finally got him noticed.

Business email compromise and other IT security issues are not the simple, easy-to-spot scams they once were. These are sophisticated, involved schemes that have devastating financial and emotional tolls on individuals and businesses.

As this story and highly public data breaches (JP Morgan, Equifax, Marriott International) show, cybercrime today is highly organized. This isn't a bunch of young hackers in hoodies. It's a thriving global business worth (conservatively) about $6 trillion per year. That kind of money lends the activities extreme sophistication. They can afford to hire graphic artists and copywriters, duplicating emails so they look nearly indistinguishable from the real deal. They use social engineering to get key personal information that makes a scam or scheme possible.

(In our security awareness training, we always warn people about stranger danger. You wouldn't tell a stranger on the street where you bank, so don't give that information to someone who calls you on the phone.)

These cybercriminals also know exactly what kind of people and companies to target. They primarily go after small businesses because they know they don't often have the same resources or security measures to protect themselves against cyberattacks. Small businesses are low-hanging fruit in the world of cybercrime. Busy, hustling business owners are prime targets. They have full permissions and access, and they might just be so rushed that they'll respond to an email without fully thinking it through.

Over the decades, I've had to sit at those conference tables and have those heart-wrenching conversations with people. People whose payroll accounts have been compromised, and they can't pay their employees. People who've lost their life savings. People who don't know how they're going to cover their utility bill, pay the mortgage, or get groceries this month because they're totally wiped out.

The statistics around the impact are equally bleak. Of the companies that lost their data for ten days or more, 93 percent ended up filing for bankruptcy within one year of the attack. A full 60 percent filed for bankruptcy immediately. Given the financial toll, that makes sense. The average ransomware attack costs a company $170,000, and the average cost of IT downtime is $5,600 per minute.

Massive organizations can often absorb those kinds of financial hits. Small companies, which cybercriminals are more prone to target, often can't.

• You Never Expect It

Just like a heart attack or any other kind of crime, you never think you're going to be the one falling victim. Until you do. One client had an employee they had to let go, and that person became incredibly vindictive. The individual made a duplicate of the company keys before returning them. Late at night, this person covertly accessed the premises and engaged in devious activities. They even simulated a cyberattack, making the organization believe they were compromised by external threats.

Upon reviewing security data and communication records, the organization was taken aback. The last person they would have suspected turned out to be the culprit. It was an emotional discovery for everyone involved and a good reminder that these kinds of attacks can happen to anyone.

- ## With Cybercrime, the Hits Keep Coming

Getting scammed has a financial ripple effect, and it goes far beyond that first hit. Losing data can cripple a business by disrupting operations, hindering decision-making, inviting legal and regulatory consequences, decreasing productivity, and compromising competitive positioning. The recovery efforts are costly and divert critical resources.

Losing your data has a similar effect. Your whole business comes to a grinding halt. Your sales team can't sell. Your accounting people can't collect. Until that data is recovered, your business can't get back up and running.

- ## You're Probably Not Getting the Money Back

One of the harshest realities about cybercrime is that your chances of getting any money back are incredibly slim. Unless you stop the transaction or alert somebody within a couple of hours, that money is likely gone.

Because these crimes often originate in other countries, there's no legal jurisdiction or recourse to get it back. You can follow the money and see where it goes, but then there are no law enforcement bodies to do anything about it.

Helping people through the emotions of realizing that money is gone is a key part of what we do.

- ## Threat Actors Aren't Going to Be Punished

Because law enforcement doesn't have jurisdiction in other countries, the threat actors, scammers, and hackers aren't usually getting pursued or caught. People think their banks or law enforcement can help. They can't. I've been in many boardrooms with people crying, swearing, or losing it when this realization hits.

Understanding the emotions that come with that lack of justice is critical to helping people move on with next steps.

- **The Changing Work Environment Makes People More Vulnerable**

With the sudden onset of remote work during the pandemic, many companies went from one head office to many little home offices. That data sprawl put lots of companies at risk. It's particularly important for remote workers to have two-factor authentication on all their accounts and to implement the same security precautions that would be used in house at every off-site micro-office. This means segregating any working environment from any personal network.

We always explain that hackers aren't attacking the secure cloud servers where everything is stored. They're attacking the individual users. Your company's security and data are only as protected as the most vulnerable person on your team.

If someone shares a work computer with a family member or leaves a laptop signed in and a visiting relative checks their email, that leaves your company open to attack.

- **Cybercrime Is Largely Preventable**

The fact that most attacks can be prevented is the hardest part of my job.

They could be prevented if:

⇨ Someone had called to double-check.
⇨ Two-factor authentication had been used.
⇨ Passwords weren't recycled.
⇨ Data had been backed up.
⇨ The password had been more secure.
⇨ There had been an air gap between the device and the backup system.
⇨ Someone didn't click something they weren't supposed to.
⇨ Someone had clicked something they were supposed to.
⇨ Security measures were put in place.
⇨ Vulnerabilities were addressed beforehand.

When these things happen, you drastically reduce your chance of being a cybercrime victim.

THE IMPORTANCE OF NETWORK ASSESSMENTS AND SECURITY AWARENESS TRAINING

Being safe in the digital era isn't always intuitive to everyone. Comprehensive network assessments and security awareness training educate organizations and individuals, empowering them with the knowledge to help prevent cyberattacks.

Companies that consistently execute security awareness training are less at risk of losing time, money, and sensitive company information. The worst-case scenario for a trained team is that someone sees a genuine email and assumes it's fraud.

Enrolling your team in proactive security awareness training and engaging in comprehensive network assessments are your greatest lines of defense against falling victim to an IT Scam.

One click is all it takes to lose a business, but luckily,
one click is all it takes to protect it.
~ Barbara Paluszkiewicz

About Barbara

Barbara Paluszkiewicz, as the visionary CEO of CDN Technologies, has not only championed the cause of top-tier IT services but has also steered the company to become the first and only CompTIA Security Trustmark+ accredited Technology Service Provider in Canada. This prestigious recognition underscores their commitment to offering impeccable IT Service, IT Support, and Cyber Security Services to small and medium enterprises across southern Ontario.

Her first book, *IT Scams: How To Avoid Being Ripped Off By Your Computer Guy And IT Services*, offers a candid look into the challenges businesses often face in the tech industry. Beyond written words, she expands on tech insights through her podcast platform, *KNOW Tech Talk*.

With three decades of experience, Barbara emphasizes that cybersecurity is about creating a stable, worry-free digital environment for businesses. This perspective, combined with her ability to demystify complex tech topics, has solidified her as a go-to expert in her field. Barbara has appeared on television networks such as ABC, NBC, CBS, City TV, ROGERS, and FOX TV, where she delves into topics ranging from ransomware threats to the importance of robust IT systems.

Her speaking engagements have also led her to the prestigious stage of Carnegie Hall, marking a highlight in her professional speaking journey. For businesses navigating the complexities of the tech landscape, Barbara Paluszkiewicz and CDN Technologies offer a guiding hand.

Get to know more at:

- www.cdntechnologies.com.

CHAPTER 13

HOW A SALESPERSON BECOMES A LEADER

BY CURT SHEWELL

As I rub the stone, I feel the slight indent worn into its surface by my thumb.

It's been sixteen years since Stephanie, our beautiful little angel, went to Heaven. This rock was from her collection, and now it sits in my pocket—always. I pull it out whenever I need to talk to God or feel Stephanie's presence.

She was eight when we learned she had aggressive brain cancer. Her three-year journey after that, her astounding resiliency, and her joy helped me become more empathetic than I thought possible. Her battle gave me perspective. It taught me how to connect with people on a more genuine level, and once I started doing that, it opened amazing leadership opportunities I never imagined.

Without those lessons, I'm not the business mentor and leader I am today. I'm not the real estate coach with more than three thousand fellow Realtors in my network. I'm not a key piece of the Z Real Estate Experts at eXp Realty, ranked among the globe's top ten real estate teams.

HOW MY MIRACLE JOB FOUND ME

I've been in sales my entire career, including regional vice-president in Honeywell's sales division. The job required me to be on the road a lot, and when Stephanie got sick, I resigned. Between endless doctor appointments and time with my family, I had to leave the workforce for a year.

Unfortunately, even when your world crumbles, the bills don't stop. One son was in college, and another was going the following year. I had a mortgage, credit card debt, and a mountain of medical bills. We were completely broke and on the verge of losing everything.
Then the doorbell rang...

Two men showed up at my house. Our family had been put forward as someone their local charity could help. I thanked them but said they couldn't possibly give us enough to make a difference.

"That bad?" one asked.

"Worse," I replied. I hauled out two overflowing milk crates. One with medical bills. The other with all other expenses. They generously offered to pay two house payments, and I couldn't help but laugh. We were three behind.

I was rational to the situation. Whatever they gave me, it wouldn't be enough. I knew other families in need would be ecstatic for that money. It would make a real difference in their lives. That wasn't us. I needed a miracle job.

One of the men perked up, "What's a miracle job?"

I told them I was in sales. I could sell anything, but I needed big-commission items. I also needed a job that was OK with me dropping everything at a moment's notice and driving nine hours to my daughter's hospital. I needed a job that would close my deals while I was gone. Pay me on time. Welcome me back with open arms after being away for six days, six weeks, or however long Stephanie needed me.

The man took a beat. "Can you give me until tomorrow?"

The next day, true to his word, his son called. The son worked for the company that built the very house we were about to lose. He had even met my wife and daughters when they were picking out cabinetry and carpets.

It turned out he was a throat cancer survivor. The doctors told him he'd never speak again, but there he was. Fifteen years into remission and fully able to speak.

"My dad told me all about your situation," he said, "and I want to do something for you."

He offered me a job selling the houses his company built. "You went through the whole experience with our company. You're the client. Just sell to people like you." He told me they worked in a partner system. If I got a call and had to be there for my little girl, I could just lock the door and call my partner. She'd take care of everything while I was away.

That was nineteen years ago. Today, I know every step that led to what I've built was part of a much bigger, more profound plan.

WHAT TRAGEDY TAUGHT ME ABOUT EMPATHY AND LEADERSHIP

I used to chase a buck. I took things for granted. I asked God for petty, naïve, immature things. Stephanie's battle changed everything. The beauty, grace, and wisdom she brought to our lives in those eleven years allowed me to become what I am today. Now I'm open to God's messages. I see the beauty I missed for so long.

I successfully manage my network of thousands of real estate agents, not because I'm anything special, but because I've been given that gift.

All my success in real estate, mentorship, and leadership has come down to these key principles:

#1. It Was Never about Me

From the moment I learned cancer was growing into Stephanie's brainstem, it stopped being about me. I put on a brave face at every doctor appointment and surgery. If I looked scared, Stephanie would be scared, and that wasn't an option.

"No matter what the doctors say or how anyone reacts, you look at me," I told her. "If I ain't worried, you ain't worried." Sitting in the hospital parking lot, she made me pinky promise on it. Then we walked in together to start the first of what would be four brain surgeries over three years.

When tragedy happens, you often find the pieces of your truest self. This journey helped me see it's not about me. When you're young, you feel like the center of the universe. Think about Christmas morning and the excitement as kids count up their presents. As you get older, the greater joy is giving and watching others receive your kindness.

Nothing is ours to keep. It's all ours to give.

#2. Stop Selling; Start Helping

After Stephanie got sick, I could relate to other people better. I saw their values and what mattered to them. I could bring genuine empathy. When I listened to them, nothing they said could scare me because I knew I could handle it.

As a salesperson, I've always known how to talk to people. I could always close. I could get people to commit and buy. I was good at it.

Now I'm amazing at it...because I don't sell anymore. I help people —honestly and genuinely. I work with real estate agents across the country, and one of my main goals is to get everyone to stop selling and start helping people. Shifting that mindset and getting agents to come from a position of helping is the single best way to increase their success.

#3. You Attract What You Put Out

The way you operate determines the kind of people who gravitate toward you. Today, I find the people swimming toward me and my boat are almost always my tribe. I attract the right people because of how I act, present myself, and treat others. In the past, this wasn't always the case. Sometimes I let the wrong people in, and it compromised my boat.

Today, I know how to judge who's a good fit for the crew. My boat—and the network of people in it—is pretty darn solid now. And if you are the wrong kind of person, you usually end up falling back into the water on your own.

#4. Leadership's a Choice

If you have authority over others, they'll follow—because they have to. True leaders are those who can inspire, even without that authority. My people would go through a brick wall for me because I would go through one for them. When I ask something difficult of them, I always go first. I'm vulnerable to them. I give them opportunities.

I don't judge them for what they've done. I know I can't change who they were, but if they let me help, I can make them better versions of themselves.

How? By choosing to lead with my heart.

#5. Put People First

I always say I don't need more money. I need more people. I chased money for thirty years, and it didn't get me far. Now I chase people. I put them first, and I help them first. Because of that, I've been able to build a more successful career than I ever imagined.

When it's just you, you sell one house and get paid once. When you empower three thousand agents to sell, you sell three thousand houses.

Prioritize *people*. Chase *people*. The money comes.

#6. Respect Is Key to Managing People

When I was twenty-four, I had my first management position at an appliance chain. Many workers there were older than me, and this role forced me to learn how to successfully manage interactions with people of all ages.

I quickly discovered that the key to managing people—or selling to them—was simple. Be courteous, helpful, and respectful. When you do that, people become easy to sell to. (They might even end up referring friends and family members to you!)

Being empathetic isn't a mystery. It's about finding a way to understand what people need. When you do that, the sales come.

#7. Your People Are Watching

As a leader, be the best possible example. Even if you don't think they are, your people are watching. When you lead with positivity, respect, and empathy, they see that, and they're more likely to follow you.

I was on the edge of losing everything material in my life. I was beyond broke. But I continued to do the right things. I treated people the right way, and those actions had powerful influence.

I come into work every day like it's the greatest day. I smile. I bring nothing but positivity because I know I'm blessed beyond anything I could have asked for. And I make sure my people see that gratitude.

#8. How You Do Anything Is How You Do Everything

Details matter.

To be a successful leader, consistently show up as a person others would follow. Ask yourself, would you follow you? If not, realize you have the ability to change that—but only if you get out of your own way. Acknowledge the problem isn't that others aren't following; it's that you're not leading.

It's not about you. Make it about your people, and you're on your way to better leadership.

#9. Create a Connection

Few people remember what you say to them. Everyone remembers how you make them feel. If you don't forge a connection with someone or make them feel anything, that relationship (and deal) aren't going anywhere. Genuine connection is the key to moving forward together. How do you quickly and authentically build that bond? By listening deeply.

Most real estate agents are so preoccupied thinking about what they're going to say next they forget to actually listen. When I'm showing houses, it doesn't matter to me which the client buys. What matters is they end up in a home they need and want. I do that by listening.

The best real estate agents are those who tell their clients nothing and ask them everything.

When you actively listen to others, you give them an unforgettable experience. When you do that, you've earned a client for life.

#10. 'No' Is Your Friend

Asking someone point blank if they're going to buy that house often turns a pleasant experience into something awkward. What would make it better for your clients? Allowing them to say no.

- Any reason you wouldn't buy this house?
- Anything that would stop you from making that offer?
- Any reason I shouldn't get on the phone with the other agent right now?

(I ask in threes to ensure I'm not inadvertently talking them into something.)

When you frame every part of the home-buying experience through the lens of what the client needs, that's when you start seeing massive success.

#11. Live a Life of Helping

Part of empathy is understanding you can't help anybody until you help yourself. I have more success now than I've ever had, and I've never been more humble. I've never been more aware that there's never a shortage of people to help.

I get to come to work every day and help thousands of clients through thousands of agents.

If that's God's plan for me, I'm all in.

SUCCESS COMES WHEN YOU PRIORITIZE HELPING OTHERS

I used to be a salesperson. The journey my family and I went through with Stephanie made me into a leader. Stephanie's battle guided me toward a more empathetic mindset, and that gave me all the tools I didn't even realize I was missing.

Today, every sales method I use has one thing in common. It's about genuinely helping people. Every interaction and decision I make is aimed at being a facilitator that gets people to what they truly need.

I use the same guiding principle in my coaching and training. I've found my passion helping real estate agents and team leaders all across the country optimize their leadership, attraction, and production.

And I know—with my clients, my Realtor network, and my family— I'll continue to do the right things. Every day. Because if I do, I'll eventually see Stephanie again, and I'm not doing anything to lose that chance.

About Curt

Curt Shewell is a distinguished author and a beacon of empathetic leadership, renowned for his remarkable journey from a personal crisis to a triumphant career in the real estate industry. The forthcoming collaborative book with Chris Voss, Empathetic Leadership, will include Curt as a contributing author. It promises to inspire and guide individuals towards creating a positive impact in their professional lives.

Joining forces with Z Real Estate in 2018 opened new horizons for Curt. He emphasizes the significance of proximity and collaboration, which allowed him to elevate his career by engaging with top leaders in the industry. His ability to swiftly build and scale teams, both locally and internationally, is a testament to his visionary leadership.

Curt's profound life experiences have instilled in him a desire to assist others during their darkest moments. He understands the significance of support when individuals are hesitant to ask for help, and he is dedicated to being there for others as they navigate through their own challenges.

Curt firmly believes that the best leaders are those who prioritize the success and well-being of others. Empathy, dedication, and selflessness are the hallmarks of his leadership style.

In Curt Shewell's view, success is measured by the number of lives one can positively impact and assist in achieving their aspirations. His guiding principle is simple yet profound: "If you help a whole bunch of people get what they want, you'll get what you want, but you have to serve first." Curt's story is an inspiring testament to the transformative power of empathy and leadership, a story that promises to resonate deeply with readers.

To reach out to Curt, visit:

- www.CurtShewell.com

CHAPTER 14

EMPATHY—THE POWER TO BREAK THE CYCLE OF POVERTY

BY MICHAEL KRAMER

I will never forget the fearful look on my mother's face when she came to me, her youngest son, twenty-one years old, number nine of her ten children, and told me she didn't have six hundred dollars to dig my father's grave. The night before, he had died on a hospital bed in our living room after a three-year battle with colon cancer that had spread to his liver. My mom, Gladys, didn't know what to do.

That day in 1992, I felt a mix of emotions, from shock and disbelief to anger to an even deeper sadness at an already difficult time. I was speechless. "How," I thought over and over that day, "does a man who had been a great dad, was well known and respected in the community, and was a business owner for over thirty years leave his wife and children broke?"

Though my dad, Cy, was my hero—I had idolized the ground he walked on and wanted to be him—dreams of one day filling his shoes as owner of the family auto business quickly faded. I learned that while my dad was a generous man, he was not a strong businessman, and it hurt my family.

At the time, I didn't know how, but I was going to find a way to right this wrong and make real money.

A LEARNING EXPERIENCE

I got a teaching degree, but after college, I ended up getting a job with a Caterpillar dealership. It was there I learned how to sell and fell in love with my customers. They were blue-collar, salt-of-the-earth business owners who used our equipment. They reminded me of Dad—except for one big difference: they drove new trucks, had boats on lakes, and had pools in their backyards. They were making money!

After a few years at Caterpillar, I decided owning a business was my answer to making real money. Every waking moment I wasn't selling equipment I spent researching business opportunities, reading business books, talking to business owners, and attending business seminars. I was going to bed thinking about business and waking up thinking about business. I was all in! I looked at everything from chiropractic to dentistry to auto body, stock trading, and home remodeling. Nothing was off-limits.

Meanwhile, my wife wished I was more available for the family and not so obsessed with buying a business and making money. Though I knew she deserved better, nothing changed, except I thought, "If I could just hurry up and get the business going, then I could spend more time with her and our kids."

Next, I bought a franchise and religiously followed the playbook. I had something to prove to myself, and to my family—that owning a business was the answer I had been looking for. In the first year, I was the fastest-growing franchise, and in the next year, I was the top-producing franchise in the country out of 150 markets. I had made it! I finally had a business and was making great money. My family's future was secure.

But my marriage wasn't. And in 2011, we divorced. I was crushed because I thought I was building the business for my family, and now all the money in the world couldn't keep us together. How did my best efforts and intentions end with divorce? I missed seeing the whole picture. I concluded I'm a good businessman, but I wasn't good in relationships.

It wasn't until I read a couple of books that the light went on for me. One of them was *Never Split the Difference* by Chris Voss. This book helped me realize I was lacking empathy in the most important relationships. And it really struck a chord with me because not only was his strategy of using empathy very logical, but it was easy to practice in business, where I thrived and results are tracked.

INVESTING IN PROPERTIES—AND PEOPLE

Our business, Freed by Real Estate, is the culmination of my desire to teach others how empathy combined with a clear business model is the key to enduring success in business and at home. Through this venture, we provide simple yet powerful tools to help others act with empathy and make money investing in the most lucrative 5 percent of properties sold, bypassing the competition for the 95 percent everyone fights over.

If I can help someone feel gratitude, believe in abundance, and act accordingly, I consider that a win for them. If I can help them apply these things to investing in real estate, I consider that a win for generations!

Twelve family members work in the business, which has four main divisions:

(1). Acquisitions, managed by my son, Luke.
(2). Rehab and Construction, which my son, Paul, runs.
(3). Property Management and Leasing, run by my daughter, Elaine, and her husband, Ben.
(4). Lending and Finance, which Luke and I run.

And my wife, Lucy, is the CFO.

Our purpose is to create generational wealth through real estate and to teach the next generation to do the same. This is not so we have our name on a building but for my family to enjoy a legacy they're proud of, to set them up for success and not failure, both in business and in life—to break the cycle of poverty.

Empathy has proved to be a huge part of our success.

HELPING OTHERS HELPS YOU

As I began to be more empathetic, I saw instant results at work. The biggest difference I noticed was in how my view of other people shifted. I used to look at people and ask myself, "What can they do for me? How can they help me?" If there wasn't a use for them in my world, then I didn't try to connect with them. This was selfish, even damaging.

Now, the way I view people is I'm curious about them. What's their story? What are they trying to accomplish, and does working with us help them do that? For example, going into a seller meeting, we are not wed to any result. We don't have a pitch or presentation for our seller. You might say, "These guys have failed to prepare, so they are prepared to fail." Don't misunderstand; we want to buy property. It's what we do. But thanks to empathy, our *how* has changed dramatically. The focus of our process has shifted to helping others get what they want.

We give them all their options, and they decide what's best for them. Before we buy a property, one of our favorite questions to ask is, "Is there anyone in your family who can benefit from owning it?" We believe real estate is a cornerstone to creating financial wealth, and that question helps remind the seller of the weight of their decision. Sometimes they end up keeping the property for their family. If they decide selling it is their best option, we ask if we can be part of it. And if we can't, we get out of their way or point them in the right direction so they can accomplish what they're trying to accomplish.

It's been amazing. You can feel the difference—it's palpable. Real estate is the business, but empathy is the *how*. As Chris Voss says, there are no guarantees of success, but if you employ empathy, you give yourself the best chance. Now I practice empathy every day in every conversation. I am continually improving as a communicator, and my relationships, business and personal, are the best I've ever had.

In our business, we practically employ empathy by talking with sellers about what we call FORD: Family, Occupation, Recreation, and Dreams. Often people will want to talk about the deal, the transaction, because it's 'what we are here to talk about,' but we have to avoid being sucked into a transaction-only conversation, or we end up acting like everyone else. We like to also talk about their family, what they do for work, what they like to do outside work, their plans for the money—all opportunities to connect with people on a deeper level. Oftentimes, the way a sale is structured comes from these conversations. It's never as simple as a contract and a check. I believe this is not only the most fruitful approach, but also the most respectful.

Empathy has changed my life so much for the better. We're approaching four hundred cash-flowing rental properties owned. Three of my four kids work full time in the business. Each own their own properties, they own some with me, and they own some with each other. We currently operate in the Midwest but are expanding nationally, and we're looking to add people to the business.

A SUPERPOWER IN BUSINESS

The example of empathy in business I'm most proud of involves my son Luke. When he was nineteen, he came to me and said he wanted to drop out of school and work in the family business. That was a hard conversation because I believe in education. But to be able to hear him out and understand what he was dealing with was huge for me. Using tactical empathy, one of Chris Voss' tools, with my son, I was able to *show* Luke I heard him by demonstrating understanding, not just say, "I understand." Once he knew I got what he was saying and feeling, we were able to talk openly, and that eventually led to him working in the business.

It would have been easy for me to give in to my frustration and say, "Go figure it out—I don't want to understand what you're trying to accomplish. I want what I want." Instead, I listened to what he was trying to accomplish. He broke down in tears; I broke down in tears. What brought us to tears is we were able, for the first time, to work through a hard situation without sweeping it under the rug, or me telling him to go figure it out himself. That's a glaring example of me and Luke in business, reaching a point of collaboration. We can work through anything, and that's what empathy does. It's like a freaking superpower in business.

Today, Luke is integral in our business. He doesn't even know how blessed his family is by his decisions. His work includes financial underwriting of deals, physical property inspections, repair budgets, acquiring funds from lenders, everything on the front side, all the way up to closing. Without his involvement, we'd be a much smaller business.

If I had remained stuck in an environment where I didn't practice empathy, my son wouldn't be working with me, wouldn't have sixty properties, and wouldn't be head of acquisitions at twenty-two years old.

THE JOY OF COLLABORATION

When our business was really taking off, showing empathy and understanding to a former accountant proved to be a positive move. We started to acquire multiple properties, forty or fifty a year, and I was trying to get clean financial statements. It seemed this accountant didn't fully understand the business and became overwhelmed. We learned after switching CPAs and the new one auditing our books that the former CPA had failed to file a previous year's tax return. I was shocked and angry! This is our family's business, our family's future relies on good financial data, and I don't need the IRS knocking on my door. This was unacceptable, and we needed it fixed, right away!

My wife and I set a meeting with the former accountant to talk it over. At the start of the meeting, we listened to him for an hour. We went into the conversation seeking understanding. We didn't browbeat him or push him. We weren't belittling. Instead, we said, "What do we do to move forward?" At the end of the conversation, he was very apologetic and committed to covering any penalty from the IRS. We didn't ask for him to do that. We simply expressed understanding about what he was dealing with—staff leaving and so on. He was admittedly overwhelmed.

When you get to that kind of moment, you reach a point of collaboration, where you say, "How do we work together to fix this?" It's so interesting, when you model this behavior and employ these tools—as we naturally all have the feeling someone's out to get us—the whole tenor of the conversation and the countenance with the other people change.

We left the conversation saying we should go have dinner together as couples. That's empathy 100 percent.

MIND-BLOWINGLY EFFECTIVE

Another example of how empathy benefited my business is related to a 65-unit apartment we were looking to purchase. The seller was asking $4 million, a great price we were happy to pay. The best part was that the purchase terms allowed us to take over an existing loan of $1.5 million at less than 4 percent interest. The challenge was that on top of that, we'd need a second, $2.5 million bank loan and $2 million in cash because the property needed work. I asked several banks for help with the second loan, but none were interested without me providing additional collateral, which I wasn't willing to do. Even though we could have assumed the first loan for under 4 percent interest, not the almost 8 percent rate of today, we were not able to come up with $2.5 million in cash to handle the purchase. I felt stuck and frustrated.

I came back to the seller and said unfortunately we're not going to be able to come up with the money. When the seller asked what I was going to do, I said we'll get out of your way so you can sell it to someone else and get what you want. He said, "No, you're the one who's going to buy this. I've gotten to know you and trust you. You're the right person." He said he'd give me a $2.5 million seller carryback loan at 6.5 percent interest-only for three years so I wouldn't have to come up with any money to buy it. I just have to come up with the $2 million for rehab.

How do you buy a 65-unit apartment complex and not write a check to buy it? It's because of empathy. Do you know what a 65-unit property does for my family's financial security? We expect it to be worth $8 million when we're done. One deal literally changed our family's financial future forever.

That's one deal over a three-year period. I want to do this over and over again, and I want to teach people how. It's so inspiring to trust empathy and lead people in a conversation that is so respectful and serving of a higher calling *and* get results.

Thanks to investing in real estate and to great teachers such as Chris Voss, no one in my family for generations to come will feel the pain of poverty.

About Michael

Michael Kramer solved the biggest problem most real estate investors face—finding good deals—specifically, the most lucrative 5% of properties that sell but never show up in the traditional listings and avoiding the 95% with competition and inflated prices.

"Using the traditional system to invest in real estate, you'll see the 95% of deals everyone sees, but you're NOT going to have access to the 5% that are sold but never publicly listed... which is where all the money is made. It shouldn't be this hard!"

Michael's passion for solving this problem has kept him awake countless nights working to perfect a system that identifies these hidden gems while sidestepping the fierce competition. Seeking to empower his son, Michael began teaching his 19-year-old, Luke, the secrets of his trade. Luke's decision to drop out of college and join the family business bore remarkable fruit!

Michael says of Luke: *"I am so proud of Luke and what he's accomplished! His courage to quit school, combined with our tools, has him earning six-figures! His passive income is great, but I am most excited about how his decision will bless his family for years to come...He's 22 now and he's already created Generational Wealth!"*

Seeing Luke's transformation, Michael realized the incredible potential to help others experience freedom too.

"If I can help someone like Luke feel gratitude, believe in abundance and act accordingly, I consider that a win for them. If I can help them apply these things to investing in real estate, I consider that a win for generations!"

Michael Kramer launched **Freed by Real Estate** to empower more people. Through this venture, they provide simple yet powerful tools to help you think differently and make money investing in the most lucrative 5% of properties, not the 95% everyone fights over.

Micheal adds:*"Everybody should have the opportunity to own income-producing real estate, and the way we do it is more fun! We get to invite people we like and trust to invest alongside us, so they get the same benefits we do and aren't stuck in this unfair 'real estate game'. Without help, they invest in the wrong real estate, or they do nothing at all..."*

Michael is on a mission to help you unlock the power of real estate to change your family's future. With his wife Lucy, they own, manage, and rehab properties in the Omaha area. They own 400 income-producing rentals. You can join Michael on this journey and pave your way to financial freedom with 'Freed by Real Estate.'

Contact Michael at:

- www.Freedbyrealestate.com
- www.linkedin.com/in/michaelkramerfbre
- www.facebook.com/GetFreedByRealEstate

CHAPTER 15

EMPATHY-DRIVEN LEADERSHIP IN ELECTRICAL CONSTRUCTION
SAFETY, TRAINING AND FAMILY VALUES

BY BRANDON LARK

There were more armadillos than people. There likely were more rattlesnakes, too, but they were hidden away in the nooks and crannies of the hot, dry and dusty landscape – and I wasn't about to hop out of my pick-up truck to count.

My job in the electrical construction industry had taken me to the Texas panhandle, where I was leading a team of 200 or so individuals to build 235 miles of high voltage line across the barren countryside. This was 'in-between' land – that is, the stretches of fields and hills *in between* the cities and towns of the Lonestar State.

It's the out-of-the-way terrain you never visit and rarely see...unless you're flying overhead in a 747...or unless you're an armadillo. Out there, there are no red lights and roundabouts, and definitely no high-priced restaurants and sprawling shopping centers.

We were constructing miles and miles of high voltage lines and transmission towers. Mind you, these *aren't* the 40-foot wooden poles that fill your average neighborhood. No, these are the colossal steel structures that carry electricity from city to city and that make the 21st-century way of life a daily reality.

Transmission towers can stretch as much as 200 feet into the sky -- five times the height of that wooden pole. Of the 700,000 miles of electric lines in the United States, more than 200,000 of them are high voltage lines. They're the interstate system of the power grid, carrying electricity over long distances of land and water in order to power everything around you, from the factory down the street to the lightbulb in the next room.

On paper, it sounds simple: transmission towers deliver electricity from the power station to the substation – they lower the voltage to the power lines in your local town and city. In reality, though, it's far more complicated.

A time traveler transported into our modern world likely would consider these towers to be silver giants roaming the landscape. Perhaps those armadillos did, too.

At the time, I was a vice president of Great Southwestern Construction, a specialty electrical contractor founded in 1977 that delivers electrical construction services to utilities, municipalities, government entities and private developers.

It was early spring in the Texas panhandle, with scorching hot days during daylight and cool crisp nights under the moonlight. We experienced plenty of postcard-worthy sunrises and sunsets: their fiery orange hues painting the dusty land with an other-worldly color. We saw plenty of armadillos, too, in addition to a few mule deer, pronghorn antelope, turkey, quail and doves. During the evening, we even heard the cries of coyotes, their haunting, high-pitched howls echoing off the bluffs and throughout the valley.

Unfortunately, though, I had little time to enjoy the scenery and wildlife. I was too busy ensuring that our shorthanded crew finished the job. We had transmission towers standing bare throughout the dusty countryside, their wires still tightly wound on their reels as they awaited a crew that had yet to be hired. Yes, some of our excuses were legitimate. (For example, an internal company crew that could have worked on our project had been overextended on a separate job due to bad weather.) But some of our excuses just didn't cut it. (We had tried to grow the company too fast, too soon.)

At 235 miles, the job was so large that I often rode in a helicopter to monitor the progress, flying high over the towers to determine our next steps. Many days, workers would get in their cars and drive 60 to 90 minutes back to their hotel. That's how far we were from the big city.

LESSONS LEARNED

The good news? We got the job done and we learned from the experience. The bad news? It placed major stress on our employees and on our company. Due to the short days of spring, we worked multiple nights under artificial lights, a last-resort step in our industry that only adds to the taxiing nature of the job.

That job in the Texas panhandle was a turning point in our company's focus. It also reinforced my passion for employee-centered empathy throughout our organization. Simply put: If employees are stretched too thin, too often, it can have a detrimental impact on their well-being and on the organization's performance. Families fall apart. Workers leave. Productivity declines. And safety suffers. If stress can cause hair loss, I lost my fair share of it back then.

I am now the president of Great Southwestern Construction, and I take seriously our motto: *People First.* I want spouses and children to have confidence their loved one is coming home safely each night. I want to see relationships and marriages not only survive but thrive. Just as I enjoy taking my three kids hiking and skiing or watching them play soccer, I want my employees to enjoy their families during those precious moments away from work. I want our employers to view their day-to-day job not as work, but as a rewarding career from which they can retire. That's how my company defines empathy.

HOW I GOT HERE

I grew up in rural New Mexico on a family-owned ranch that was picturesque but also too small to fully support a family. My parents held jobs away from home – my dad as a carpenter in the construction business and my mom in accounting. They instilled in me a strong moral compass and a desire to earn an honest dollar. They taught me that your word should be stronger than any written contract. With hard work, they said anything is possible. A good leader, they told me, is also a good servant.

As a boy, I always had an interest in building and creating. With my dad in the industry, a career in construction only seemed natural. After high school, I got an associate's degree in civil engineering, and after that, I joined the crew of a high voltage electrical contractor. I climbed the ranks, from entry level to field supervision, and now in management. I joined Great Southwestern Construction more than two decades ago. In the middle of all that, I also earned a bachelor's degree and an MBA – two degrees supported by my employer.

Everyone on my leadership team has spent time in the trade. As we've discovered, it's easier to be empathetic with employees when you've walked a mile in their shoes. I've stood out in the scorching sunshine, its rays mercilessly beating down on myself and my co-workers. I've helped erect the types of high voltage towers and lines that I am now overseeing. When you've shared the same experiences, you're better able to understand an employee's concerns and struggles.

At Great Southwestern Construction, safety is not simply a priority; safety is life. It means more than having the best training and best equipment. Safety is a perpetual mindset woven into our attitudes, values, objectives and actions. You can't have safety in electrical construction without a laser-like focus on empathy. One requires the other. One *leads to* the other.

We've been a field leader in safety, embracing new technologies and new practices that ensure our employees not only feel safe but are safe. According to data from the U.S. Bureau of Labor Statistics, the number of nonfatal injuries nationwide on electrical work in 2018 – in all private electrical work – was one-fourth what it was more than two decades earlier in 1994. Fatal injuries also have plummeted nationwide, hitting record lows and near-record lows from 2013 onward. (From 2004 to 2020, they declined more than 50 percent.)

No doubt, electrical construction, by its very nature, carries risks. But by ingraining a safety-first mentality from top to bottom, and by encouraging honest communication across the board, we can give employees the confidence they need to complete the task. We also can give their spouses and children peace of mind.

MAKING SAFETY THE HIGHEST PRIORITY

Here's one example: Years ago, men and women on the field would 'free climb' structures, from the bottom to the top, without safety belts, thus endangering not only themselves but also their co-workers down below. It was a common industry-wide practice born out of naivety and ego that led to numerous accidents. (Something as simple as a wet shoe could spell tragedy.)

Today, such practices are not only frowned upon but banned. When a lineworker begins climbing a pole nowadays, he or she must be strapped to the structure, from beginning to end. Yes, there was initial resistance to this new, safer practice. ("You're slowing us down; you're going to kill the industry!" opponents shouted.) But a company cannot claim to be safety-driven, and empathetic if it lets its employees follow unsafe practices. Eventually, everyone bought into the new rules. We explained how it benefits not only their own personal safety but also the company's health and growth. For safety to be truly rooted in the culture, it must be embraced and promoted by everyone: managers, supervisors and field workers, alike. In this industry, you are your brother's keeper; you look out for each other, care for each other, and ensure that your colleagues go home just as they arrived. I often challenge people I encounter: What will you do today to send people home *better* than they arrived?

Here's another example of this safety-first approach: We encourage employees to speak out – to raise their hand, so to speak – about their safety concerns. We even give rewards to the employees who offer the most significant suggestions. The goal is for employees to overcome their natural reluctance to confront authority. We don't want to 'let things slide.' Instead, we want to avoid accidents before they happen.

Empathy requires innovative solutions that bring us closer to a workplace where harm is minimized. Empathy also requires that we are committed to the company's success and, by extension, the development of each employee. In recent years, we have dramatically increased the training that is required before a new worker is given more responsibilities.

In this industry, knowledge and experience can be the difference between life and death. We often ask our employees about their personal lives, not only because we care about their mental and emotional wellbeing, but also because we care about their safety on the job. If they're facing a trial or tragedy at home, we can assign them tasks that require less thought and are more safe. That's a complete shift from how it was done decades ago, when you showed up, signed the paperwork, and started on the job – no questions asked. Today, we place mentors alongside newbies. We closely watch their day-to-day actions.

LOOKING TOWARD THE FUTURE

For long-time employees, we regularly offer new training. We remind them of what's required but we also teach them new, safer practices. It's like a baseball team at Spring Training with a mix of old and new players. We want our veterans to come alongside the rookies and guide them. We want our first-year employees to grow into all-stars. Just as important, we want our team to gel into an empathy-driven cohesive unit that encourages and supports one another. Much like a championship baseball team, we want employees to be their brother's keeper.

A company that leads with empathy places families first. Sadly, that wasn't the case when I first got into the industry. Back then, it was assumed you'd be married three times and divorced three times – and that the house you built would be passed on to your ex. Fortunately, the industry has seen a major overhaul in its focus on home life, just as it's seen a major revolution in safety. I personally am committed to my wife and children and, therefore, understand that there will be times when employees will need to take time to focus on their family, too.

Finally, an empathy-centric company also cares for the next generation. For several decades, high school students have been told – wrongly – that the only path to success runs through college. The result: mountains of debt and countless graduates with no jobs. Consider this: 68 percent of high school students enter college, yet each year 40 percent of undergraduates leave their institution of higher learning.

Even worse, only 27 percent of college graduates say they are working in a field related to their degree. It's paramount for our society to have an honest conversation about the paths high school students are offered. Great Southwestern Construction is committed to giving high school graduates an option that doesn't shackle young adults with debt and instead offers them a rewarding trade career that will benefit them for life.

FINAL THOUGHTS

Empathy is essential to the growth of the company – yes – but also to its employees and their families. It's the glue that bonds the team and makes it strong. Without it, the company falls apart. But with it, we can build powerful connections that foster a sense of unity, trust and mutual support among colleagues.

Austrian doctor Alfred Adler once described empathy as: "seeing with the eyes of another, listening with the ears of another, and feeling with the heart of another." That's how I view it, too.

About Brandon

Brandon Lark was appointed President of Great Southwestern Construction in May 2014 and is responsible for devising and leading the overall growth and operational strategies of Great Southwestern. Brandon joined the Company in 2000 as a Substation Superintendent, assuming increasing responsibility throughout his tenure including the positions of Project Manager, Project Developer, Senior Project Manager and Vice President. He also serves on the Executive Management Committee for MYR Group, developing and executing corporate strategy while managing enterprise risk.

Brandon blends his hands-on combination of field and project management expertise when working alongside project and operations managers repeatedly delivering successful on-time, under-budget, project execution. He has extensive experience in transmission, substation and wind farm electrical construction on projects throughout the west and southwest.

Brandon embraces the mission, vision and values of the organization and, united with his personal values and leadership philosophy, these form his foundation for success. At the core of his philosophy is steadfast focus on employee development, which allows for continuous performance improvement and also generates innovative, enhanced service offerings.

Brandon Lark has both a Bachelor of Science and Master of Business Administration (MBA) in Project Management. He also has an Associates of Science Degree in Civil Engineering Technology and is a certified Project Management Specialist. Brandon has continued his education through the MIT Sloan Executive Education, Harvard Professional Development, The Center for Creative Leadership and Academy Leadership programs, as well as many in-house training programs with both technical and leadership curriculums.

In his time away from the office, Brandon enjoys spending time with his wife and three children. His wife is an IFBB professional bodybuilder and his youngest son is an aspiring ballet student. When not watching ballet, many weekends are spent in the gym that the couple owns, working with athletes on their bodybuilding team, or supporting his wife or other athletes in competitions.

CHAPTER 16

CHANGING PERCEPTIONS, CHANGING LIVES

BY ROSBEL SERRANO-TORRES

The frightened woman was shouting at the top of her lungs, her voice echoing off the lofty ceilings and marble walls of the massive, jam-packed museum...but no one knew her language. I remember that day as if it were yesterday. I can still hear her panicked voice. I can still see the fear in her face, her eyes.

Moments earlier, visitors had been enjoying a casual stroll through the museum on a postcard-worthy, sunny Sunday afternoon in Washington, D.C. Outside, thousands of tourists were taking in the Cherry Blossom Festival, the annual event that celebrates everything we love about spring: warm sunshine, new beginnings and, of course, tree blossoms. It was a canvas in real life – millions of pink and white petals dancing slowly in the breeze against the backdrop of green grass, a blue sky and white puffy clouds sailing across the horizon.

I was a volunteer that day at the museum, full of hope and cheer and ready to assist anyone who needed help. Patrons were smiling. They were laughing. Yet the mood quickly changed when the woman's screeching voice broke the air. I had learned multiple languages during my teenage years, yet...even I couldn't understand what she was saying. No one could understand her.

She looked quickly in my direction and then in the opposite direction, seemingly unaware she was causing a scene. A few families walked out, not wanting to keep their children around. Other families stared in disbelief, not sure what to do. Still another person shouted, "Security!" Then a colleague of mine spoke up: "I think she's deaf." Deaf?

My colleague slowly approached the woman, signing a few words with her hands until the woman calmed down and responded back. She was deaf! The woman – we soon learned – had misplaced her child. That's why she was panicking. That's why she was shouting. Thankfully, the story had a happy ending – her child was in another part of the room, just out of her eyesight. They soon reunited. And the rest of us learned a valuable lesson about rushing to judgment.

That day was a turning point in my life. I embarked on a journey to learn sign language. I grew to understand empathy in a new light. I also founded Sales2Bloom, a company that helps technology organizations and salespersons grow their businesses with consistency and productivity through enterprise sales coaching and business consulting. The lessons from that day are regularly applied at Sales2Bloom.

As I've learned over the years, empathy has many forms, but it's far easier to practice in real life if you have two other elements, (1) curiosity, and (2) trust. Without curiosity, your empathy with the other person will go only so far. And without trust, your empathy will lack the "glue" that allows two people to bond. Let me explain.

THE IMPORTANCE OF CURIOSITY

Encouraging curiosity within yourself and those around you can transform how you view the world. The more you're curious, the more likely you are to want to learn about people – their cultures, their talents, their habits. (Curiosity is one reason I have learned a total of seven languages.) It has other benefits: Curiosity can improve your decision-making and your innovation. It can lead to heightened understanding and increased insight.

Psychologist Carol Dweck says that the adoption of a 'growth mindset' allows for the development and nurturing of any skill or intelligence. I am convinced that curiosity plays a pivotal role in fostering this growth mindset. Ultimately, curiosity can help you become the extraordinary leader you were meant to be.

If you believe you lack the qualities of a leader, then hold tight, because you're bound to both inspire and guide others. Leaders are rarely 'born.' Instead, most of us develop the necessary traits to become one. My childhood was marked by a fortunate upbringing that instilled in me a courageous outlook on life. Despite lacking leadership skills during my childhood and teenage years, my parents' relentless energy and attention encouraged me to always:

1) Be practical. In other words, act pragmatically and avoid analysis paralysis.
2) Think before talking. They wouldn't let me complain if I had not taken into consideration the full context of the subject, conducted the appropriate research and/or brought proposals as to what I would do next.
3) Put others first. Of course, this involves family and loved ones, but it can also involve others around us.

Like fertilizer in a garden, these three lessons were the nourishing 'stimulant' that turned me into a person who is always asking questions, who is always wondering how things work. I'm telling you – curiosity will make you unstoppable.

Consider the incident with the deaf woman. That emotion-laden episode triggered my curiosity about deaf culture, which led me to learn sign language, which, in turn, led me to volunteer work with a Mexico-based NGO helping deaf people finish their schooling. Although most of them were children, some were adults. We taught them to do things the world would say are impossible – speaking words and singing songs, among them. One man, age 55, had never articulated a single vocal word in his life. As soon as he felt the vibrations of his voice, he started crying. I nearly cried, too.

I remember being shocked by the students' lack of knowledge about their surroundings in spite of their eagerness to learn. Most students, for example, couldn't name their own country (Mexico), much less find it on a map. But I was driven to help them because I knew their context (they grew up deaf, often isolated and without resources) and because

I felt empathy for their community. Some had overprotective parents. Others grew up in a home that had little confidence in their abilities. (I learned of one couple who never took their deaf daughter out into the world. Incredibly, friends of the family didn't know she existed!)

Soon, the students in my class learned basic geography, and soon thereafter, they were using maps with ease. We even had inspiring, lively discussions about worldwide leaders, Nelson Mandela and Malala Yousafzai, among them. My curiosity about life sparked *their* curiosity.

None of this would have happened without curiosity. Curiosity can benefit you, too. The more curious you are about the people, places and things around you, the more you will learn and the more empathetic you will become.

YOUR BIOLOGY IN LEADERSHIP

Every person can grow their curiosity. Every person can be a leader. Don't believe me? Then consider your biology. You already have what it takes to develop the skills you need to lead others with empathy.

Let's take a moment to examine the biology that makes you so powerful. I promise: This quick science class will be worth it!

1. Your brain is geared for learning.

Your brain's ability to learn, re-organize and form new connections has no limit throughout your entire life. This means you can keep expanding the information and relations stored in your brain, no matter your age. You may learn a new skill, develop new habits, enhance your memory and improve your communication to cultivate meaningful relationships. You can grow your curiosity and develop a lifestyle of learning.

It's common to think of leaders as smart, but this does not always equal a high IQ. Good leaders are strong in both intrapersonal and interpersonal intelligence. Intrapersonal intelligence refers to the ability to comprehend one's own actions, cognitive processes and emotions, while interpersonal intelligence pertains to the ability to interact and understand others. Here's the good news: You can learn and develop both types of intelligence throughout your life. The ultimate key lies in deliberate practice – and not just any practice, but intelligent and purposeful practice.

2. You can learn to control your emotions.

Emotions are powerful. They can help build a relationship... or quickly tear it down. It's essential that we are intentional in understanding not only our emotions but the emotions of others. By learning about the emotions and its reactions, you will better understand others and better tailor your messages. Specifically, it's essential you realize that: a) emotions can generate stress; b) emotions can cause you to make decisions that your "rational" mind would not; and, c) emotions can divert you from your objective and cause you to lose focus when facing crucial conversations.

Learn to control your emotions by practicing conscious self-detection and self-regulation.

3. You can control your stress – I promise.

Your body wasn't designed to live with stress, but you can easily combat stress through a healthy lifestyle. Eat well, sleep well, get some exercise and learn a few activities that comfort your mind and soul. Contrary to conventional wisdom in the business world, you cannot 'get ahead' by continually cutting corners in this area of your life. More than likely, you'll eventually hit a wall and fall behind.

Notice how all three biological elements are tied together. By controlling your stress, you can better control your emotions and remember what you've learned. Your conversations with others will be more productive. A healthy lifestyle makes it easier to lead with curiosity and empathy.

Lastly, controlling stress will let you – and whoever you're interacting with – produce more oxytocin, a hormone that can be vital for empathetic leadership. Neuro-economist Paul Zak found that oxytocin generates trust and fosters empathy. This theory has been tested in different regions and cultures, including among the indigenous people of Papua New Guinea.

THE SIGNIFICANCE OF TRUST

The business world was built on trust. When we purchase a product from a store, we often do so because we trust the company, the product or because someone we trust recommended it. This same principle applies to people. When we trust others – be it personally, professionally or commercially – we do so based on a pattern of past trust.

Empathy is tied directly to trust. Let me show you why.

Author Malcolm Gladwell says we humans are hardwired to trust others because it is rooted in our evolutionary history in order to increase our chances for survival. Trust is essential for social cohesion and interaction. Without trust, cities never would have been built. The same goes for neighborhoods. (No one willingly lives near liars and thieves.) The hardest part, though, is maintaining trust. When you lose it, it's often lost for good.

If you lack trust, it's nearly impossible to lead others, whether it's a child, student, colleague or potential client. This is a subject close to my heart because I've been in enterprise sales and in customer-facing tech company consulting for several years. There, empathy and trust are vital.

In order to close deals and make a business grow, you must build trust in the product, in the company, in the team, and most importantly, in you as a consultant or salesperson. A good way to earn and maintain trust is by following these three keys:

(i). Develop a genuine interest to help others. With that interest, you will grow the desire to learn more and read more about the topic. That will give you the energy you need to take action.

(ii). Make a good connection. Show interest in the other person's needs and problems. This doesn't mean you must be friends with everyone, but instead that you have a solid, trustworthy relationship. Besides, you'll know which ones you should dedicate more time to as time passes. As Maya Angelou once wrote, "People will forget what you said, people will forget what you did, but people will never forget how you made them feel."

(iii). Ask relevant questions. Show intentional and genuine interest. Your goal is to help them talk and inform you about their feelings.

CHANGING PERCEPTIONS BY CHANGING OUR APPROACH

Remember the deaf students? To this day, one particular pupil stands out. She was in her mid-tweens with long black hair and a solemn face. Her pessimistic nature contrasted greatly with my you-can-do-anything outlook. She and I just didn't get along, even though we shared an identical language and culture. Talking to her was like talking to a wall.

But that soon changed. We organized a kayaking getaway -- a trip that had the goal of changing the students' self-image. None of them had ever done anything this adventurous. A few of them seemed nervous. Their faces were filled with apprehension. Still, they *trusted* us. They also were curious.

When they finished kayaking on the river on that bright sunny day, their moods had changed. That teenage girl looked at me with a wide smile and a sparkle in her eyes as if to say, "Thanks. I didn't know I could do that." A few of the teachers cried. We even learned that one of the students whose younger brother is a competitive rower had never been in a boat!

This life-changing adventure didn't take place in a big city. It took place in a rural area because a few adults wanted to make a difference. They wanted to lead with empathy. The students overcame their fears and self-doubt. They saw their self-image transformed, simply because a few people drastically changed their approach.

The students walked away that day with an optimistic outlook on life. They walked away wondering: What else can we do that we didn't think we could do?

I, too, learned a powerful lesson that day: Don't limit yourself...and don't limit others. Since then, I have focused on developing new skills in the people around me without prejudging what they can do. Much like a spring garden filled with a thousand seeds, I want everyone in my circle of life to bloom.

A life of empathy can open doors to countless possibilities if you dare to take a step forward and look inside. But to reach your potential, you need to walk with curiosity. You need to develop trust. Are you ready to take action toward fulfilling your life's purpose?

To put it another way: *What else can you do that you didn't think you could do?*

About Rosbel

With over 16 years of experience in driving business growth, Rosbel Serrano-Torres, as the founder of Sales2Bloom, helps tech companies find their best route to scale with consistency and productivity through enterprise sales coaching and business consulting.

Asides from corporate world experience, Rosbel has immersed in the entrepreneurial life – from selling as a kid, creating and developing multiple projects in her teens, and founding two companies. Rosbel holds a Master of Science in Telematics Engineering and a deep expertise in AI (artificial intelligence), BI (business intelligence), e-commerce, and cybersecurity domains. The mix of both business and tech has enhanced her teams to be more successful and empathetic among multiple departments.

Rosbel is a strong believer in the power of empathy to create positive change, and a strong advocate for diversity and inclusion. She believes that a diverse workforce is a more innovative and creative workforce, and is a professional who is not afraid to stand up for what she believes in. Enforcing empathy and diversity, Rosbel speaks over five languages to better connect with different cultures.

Rosbel has spoken at events in multiple cities dealing with diversity and business leadership. As a sales and business coach, she mentors a proven methodology to sell consistently, which has been successful in economic downturns and scaling to $1B+ valuation. Rosbel thrives in multicultural environments and has worked with diverse teams across the globe, from China to Russia, India, France and Brazil, among others.

Here are some things that others say about Rosbel:

"Rosbel is an achiever, open to dialogue and a hard-working professional. I totally recommend her to work on any team to upgrade your sales goals, either for LATAM or International markets. She's always helping you to understand with patience and critical thinking."

"Rosbel is a sales professional, independent, a self-starter, and very organized. I was impressed by the fact that she is always looking for ways to help; she is definitely a great team player. Rosbel has a strong background in biometrics and IT, which allows her to generate new opportunities and novel use cases."

After living in four countries, Rosbel currently lives in Mexico City where she enjoys weekend getaways to spend time in nature, while maintaining an active life; sometimes including day hikes of over 30 kilometers (18 miles) or biking over 90 kilometers (55 miles). Also, she is book-bosomed, especially inclined to read historic novels or non-fiction books. She also enjoys playing the piano and listening to music.

If you are a sales leader or director at a B2B tech company who is concerned about achieving results consistently, while developing over-achievers and purposeful teams, Rosbel is your contact.

You can contact Rosbel by connecting via:

- linkedin.com/in/rosbel
- www.sales2bloom.com

CHAPTER 17

EMPATHY BUILDS A STRONGER TEAM

BY DEREK GAUNT

Leading a team can be tough. Different personality types clashing, egos competing. It takes conscious effort to manage a group with varying degrees of experience and communication skills. You already know this.

Now, imagine a team whose members *want* to follow an order versus being *made* to – a team that other leaders notice and are undeniably impressed by. I formed and led teams like this for years during my time as a hostage negotiation team commander in the Washington DC, metropolitan area. My team members knew, regardless of the role they played, their input was valued and could impact the outcome. I created an environment where I could call up the people who worked for me and say, "Tomorrow morning, team, we're assaulting the gates of hell." And their response was, "Whose car should we take?" At the word "go" – despite personal disagreements or unresolved issues – we were a well-oiled machine. And we'd better be because lives were on the line.

So, let me ask you, does your team operate this way? I'd like to offer you some suggestions you may not have considered. Maybe you've already heard some of this but weren't at a place to give it your full attention, but now a job loss or poor evaluation has you open to change. By incorporating these leadership tools, you can systematically build a team others will strive to emulate.

I have to be honest. What I'm about to share with you, many leaders won't be able to pull off. Oh, they're capable, but there is one thing that will hold them back: sheer laziness. Because showing empathy and listening deeply is exhausting work. That's why most leaders won't do it.

My colleague Sandy was once involved in a negotiation that resulted in her being on the phone with a gunman for 10 hours. She later told me that after the event, she went home and slept for 18 hours straight. Listening with empathy takes effort. That's also why the majority of leaders aren't as successful as they could be.

How do I know this? Because early in my career, I didn't always take the time to listen empathetically. I didn't always read the cues team members sent me that would have let me know they needed help. I made mistakes. Yeah, I said it. Good leaders don't try to hide this. We're humans, not robots, and we mess up. Your team will forgive your imperfections as long as you own them, and you'll be a stronger leader because of it.

I'm going to offer up four tenets to help you build a team of people who willingly get the job done. A team who is jacked up to get to work each morning, who know their input is valued, and who share a mutual trust in you, their leader, and in their team members, despite disagreements. I'll give you a little hint: empathy plays a large role in each of them.

TENET #1: LEAD WITH HUMILITY

I had a great role model for leadership. Her name is Robyn. Robyn was an outstanding supervisor throughout her career, primarily because of how she treated her people. Now don't get it twisted, when you screwed up, she let you know it, and you were going to feel her wrath. But she had a high tolerance level, so by the time she flipped that switch, you had it coming.

Most leaders just want to meet the minimum requirements; they don't necessarily want to be outstanding. But she went the distance. Little things like legitimately acknowledging jobs well done instead of offering hollow praise. Or saying, "Hey, I know you worked until midnight last night. Why don't you come in at 10 today, instead of instead of 7, and I won't charge you with personal time." She never entered a crime scene and started telling people what to do. She knew she had competent people working for her. One of the most important lessons I took from her was that wielding your power in people's faces is unnecessary.

Hostage negotiators, SWAT operators, they're A types. These men and women bring a lot of intelligence and motivation to the table. As the commander for the team, no one was confused about who had the ultimate say, so I had no reason to carry myself in a way that screamed, "What I say goes" because it was self- evident. Besides, if you have to remind your direct reports that you're in charge, what you're actually saying is, "I'm insecure in my role as leader."

I also never gave the appearance that I was making decisions in a vacuum. So even though I carried the rank of lieutenant, and the people who worked for me carried the rank of detective, sergeant, or officer, they all knew I wanted their input during training evolutions or live events. I knew the direction I was leaning in to resolve an incident, but to assume the folks who work for me didn't have valid input sends a demoralizing message that I don't trust them. Dismissing them creates negative emotions and negative dynamics within the team, which impede everyone's ability to function at the highest level.

Many leaders don't recognize that the minute someone gets pumped up with negative emotions is the same minute their cognitive abilities are diminished. When emotions are high, rational thinking and performance are low. The message to your team should be: *I may be your boss, but I rely on you.*

TENET #2: TRUST

If you don't trust your team, I can say unequivocally, the problem isn't them. It's you. Micromanagers are insecure. They think, *If I defer to my team and something goes wrong, the buck stops with me.* This mindset creates an environment where that leader's reputation is on the line. That fear leads to micromanaging. The micromanaging leader wants their peers and those above them to believe they're the right person for the job. They've got to put their hands on everything. Meanwhile, what kind of reaction do the direct reports have for being micromanaged? Resentment. Anytime you say, through words or actions, that you don't trust someone to do their jobs, you will breed resentment. Most people won't stand for this and eventually, they'll either find another job or they'll do the Quiet Quitting move, where they're physically present but they've checked out mentally.

Many organizations have leaders who fail upward. Test-takers who get promoted rapidly. They spend their professional time reaching for the next rung of the ladder, stepping over dead bodies when necessary. In the law enforcement space, we'll have a person get promoted to the rank of sergeant and instead of learning what it means to be a frontline supervisor at that rank, they start preparing themselves to get promoted to the rank of lieutenant. They're elevated based on 'book' knowledge and connections, not on their ability to relate to people, which is learned, in essence, at the front-line level.

We should be hiring and promoting people with above-average interpersonal communication skills. Organizations say these skills are important and yet most don't model them. Don't micromanage. Trust your team to their jobs. *Train them up and then get out of their way.*

TENET #3: BE INCLUSIVE

Getting input sends the message that even though I'm the commander of the team, I'm not the smartest guy in the room. In hostage situations, we're trying to save lives, so I wanted to hear every idea. During a timeout, I'd leave the command bus, gather my team, and ask them, "Where were we? Where are we? Where do we want to go?" Then I'd listen. They may come up with something I hadn't thought about.

We were once called to an apartment complex because deputies were being threatened by a resident who was being evicted. He'd barricaded himself in his apartment, literally nailing two-by-fours across the front door. He told us his apartment was full of valuable items and he'd brewed up some caustic substance he purported was acid. We were negotiating with this guy by phone and during a break in the action, we took a timeout. One of the negotiators assigned to intelligence-gathering had pulled the resident's file at the rental office.

He said, "I have an idea. His file is full of his complaints against the complex and management. Each led to him being granted special dispensation, like reduction in rent or a premium parking space. Any time he complained, management would say, 'Give him something to make him shut up.'" The negotiator said, "Nobody's ever told this guy no. We need to flip the script on him."

The minute we got back on the phone, we told the resident, "We've given you every opportunity to direct your own decision-making and you fail to do it." The minute he recognized his manipulation wasn't going as far as he thought, he conceded. "What do you want me to do?" "Go get a crowbar and take down those two-by-fours because we're coming in regardless, and if we come in, all those expensive items will be negatively impacted." That's a nice way of saying, "You're going to eat a boatload of gas and we're probably going to break your stuff."

Imagine if I'd said to my intelligence gatherer, "Nah, I don't think that's the best route. Let's go with my idea." Then I've got an employee who's thinking, *Man, why bother, if he is going to do what he wants anyway? I've got a boss who just gives me orders and doesn't demonstrate that he understands how it's going to impact me. He's not offering any explanation. He's just saying no.*

This stings for the employee. Revenge being as powerful as it is, given the opportunity, he may do something within the parameters of remaining professional, to ensure I feel the same level of discomfort that he felt. Which would you rather have, a willing employee who follows an order because they feel like it or a disgruntled person who's going to be passive-aggressively compliant?

There are situations, though, where I give a direct order that brooks no discussion. That only occurs in situations when circumstances are exigent, meaning we got to move now. Retired US Army Lieutenant Colonel, Director of Command and Leadership Studies at the US Army War college, George Reed, had a great quote. "When the enemy is inside the wire, and you're passing out the last rounds of ammunition, decorum and deference go out the window."

The problem is that the enemy is inside the wire only a small percentage of the time, but some leaders conduct themselves in that forceful leadership style 100% of the time.

TENET #4: USE TACTICAL EMPATHY

Empathy is demonstrating you understand what the lay of the land looks like from another's perspective. It's as simple as that. Understand, in a leadership role, whether you're a frontline manager or a C-suite executive, you make decisions that impact other people and sometimes that impact is negative. The best leaders demonstrate that they understand how certain decisions affect the people tasked with doing the work.

Remember when I said practicing empathy was exhausting? It's why a lot of leaders just bypass having a discussion and go straight to: "Here's what I need you to do." because the discussion will be replete with negative emotions and those make everyone uncomfortable. So why bother? I'll tell you why. Because that person you just ordered to complete a task wasn't given the chance to offer input or didn't have any context about why it's important. You never stopped to understand how the person felt when you just demanded they do it. Naturally, this person wants to stay gainfully employed, so they comply. But they're doing it with some reluctance. Odds are high they aren't putting their best foot forward.

We all have an innate desire for someone else to understand our circumstances and environment. We don't get that need filled enough. We send signals to other people that are often missed or ignored. So, when someone comes along who is willing to fill that need, positive changes occur in the brain, but it can be emotional.

Once, one of my officers was late to roll call, which starts promptly at 3:00 so you better arrive at 2:59. If you walk in late, everybody sees it. The lieutenant beside me obviously noticed and expected me to deal with it.

I brought her into the office and asked why she couldn't get to work on time. "My car wouldn't start. And it was hot last night, so I didn't get much sleep. Our air conditioner went out...it was just a rough night."

The way she said it, my intuition told me something else was going on. I asked her if she was okay. "Yeah, I'm okay," but she said it in a tone that was flat, devoid of emotion. Her response said one thing and her tone said another. Now I had to address the disconnect between her words and behavior.

"It sounds to me like there's something else going on." With that, she completely came apart. In addition to the air conditioning and the car, there was the dog and troubles in her relationship. And as a newer officer, she was performing on the low-end, so add struggles at work. All this came out because I was curious about why her words didn't match her tone. But the scarier part was, she went from almost inconsolable to, "But I'm okay." Her emotion ceased, her face hardened – just like that. She said, "I'm going to hit the street (start her shift)."

"No, you're not." I was not going to send her out on the street in that state. I sent her home to decompress.

Leaders who fail to address behavior and words that contradict do so at their own peril. People rarely say what they mean. They ask terrible questions. They make false statements. When you can articulate something they cannot or will not articulate for themselves, this is a clear demonstration of Tactical Empathy.

———≈———

Leaders, open up a window between you and your employee where you can focus on sharpening interpersonal communication skills: listen deeply, have self-control, show empathy, grow emotional intelligence… We all want to be part of a team that performs at a higher level.

While we can't avoid making difficult decisions, especially those we know will negatively affect our employees, we can lead with humility, we can work to build trust so employees have the freedom to do what they were hired to do. We can ask for input so creative solutions are found, and practice showing empathy by taking the time to understand how our request impacts the employee. These tenets will lay a firm foundation for a first-rate team that, when the alarm sounds, will spring into action and successfully achieve the objective.

About Derek

Derek Gaunt is a negotiation coach and trainer at the Black Swan Group, and author of the leadership book: *Ego, Authority, Failure.* During his nearly 30-year law enforcement career, he served as a leader and commander of the hostage negotiations teams in the Washington, DC metropolitan area.

Early in his law enforcement career, after being selected as a detective in the Criminal Investigations Section of a municipal police agency, Derek discovered a passion for interpersonal communications skills. He spent the majority of his law enforcement career in this section as a detective, supervisor, and the commander of major crimes.

In 1997 he took his passion for interpersonal communications to the next level and became a hostage negotiator. Once promoted to supervisor, his passion transitioned to teaching negotiation concepts to others. As a hostage negotiation and incident command expert, Derek frequently speaks at negotiation and SWAT conferences across the United States.

Derek has trained teams and individuals throughout and around the world, instructing organizations on how to apply hostage negotiation practices and principles to their business. Derek presents both seminars and in-house training programs focusing on teaching techniques for understanding human behavior and navigating difficult conversations. He has been a negotiation coach with the Black Swan Group for nearly 15 years.

When Derek isn't working, he's actively pursuing one of his other passions—coaching basketball.

CHAPTER 18

THE EMPATHY IN DETERMINATION

BY JARRETT ROBERTSON

A WEALTH OF WISDOM IN EIGHTY-SEVEN CENTS

If we're very lucky, our lives are filled with people whose influence serves as a guiding light. Just knowing them makes us bigger, stronger and better versions of ourselves.

I'm thinking of the family members and schoolteachers when we're younger. They are the life mentors who come along when we need them and help shine a bright light on our path forward. As a former professional athlete coming off of a long career, I've had my share of coaches, many of those helping to develop me into a better player on the ice and teammate in the locker room.

But when I reflect on empathy and understanding, there is one mentor that stands out to me above all others, Pete Gillespie.

When I was first trying to break into the highly competitive industry of financial services, I sorely needed guidance. I was raw and unfinished. I had just finished a ten-year career in hockey, and I responded well to what you might call tough love. Pete provided that for me. He wasn't shy about getting in my ear and pushing me to get better at my job. He demanded that I strive for excellence instead of merely getting by.

Looking back, he never candy-coated anything. But Pete wasn't merely some hard-nosed, coach-like figure in my life, barking at me from the sidelines to get better. He offered a motivator even more important than tough love. He recognized how hard I was working and intuitively understood that if he offered me the necessary praise for that, as well, I would respond positively.

I remember helping my very first client secure an account. It was a college education plan and they decided they would commit twenty-five bucks a month to fund it. I had finally broken through. I was stoked and I went to tell Pete. After all of the training, coaching and advice, I wanted him to be there to help celebrate what felt like a victory.

"How much is my commission?" I asked.

Pete cracked a smile and said, "Eighty-seven cents."

I was shocked. Eighty-seven cents? For all of that work, I was set to take home less than the cost of a cup of coffee. But Pete would not let me hang my head.

"Great job," he said.

He slapped me on my back and took the time to compliment how I handled the client. He pointed out how I had properly completed the necessary paperwork. I felt like I had just secured a million dollar sale. Pete understood, when it came to a first victory, it wasn't the amount of money that mattered to me. It was about getting over the hump. I walked out of that meeting happy and, more than anything else, ready to take the next step.

HUMBLE BEGINNINGS

Pete gave me everything I needed to get started in this business. It is only through the grace and guidance of his abundant empathy that I am here today, telling this story as a success in my field. I was pretty rough around the edges when I was just starting out. After retiring from a career in hockey that carried me through most of my twenties, I wasn't really sure how the world of business worked. I needed an example. I needed someone who could be my mentor.

Every office has a guy like Pete. He was the kind of guy who came in first thing in the morning, around seven, at his desk before most anyone else. I didn't know much, but I realized that I wanted to meet that standard, so I started getting up around five o'clock, got my workout in, and put my meals together. Athletics and fitness were still very important to me.

Since I was in downtown Toronto, I would take the streetcar to the train, commuting for more than an hour, only to come staggering into the office. I was a mess. I only had the one shirt and tie because, just starting out, I didn't have much money to spend on clothes. Pete didn't see the rough edges though. I didn't know anything except that I was hungry, eager to learn the ropes, and somehow, for him, that was all that seemed to matter.

Looking back, I think I would have probably quit the business if it wasn't for Pete's tutelage. He was such a good and patient listener. He really took the time needed to get to know me, to understand what worked for me and what didn't. He found ways to get me motivated. He picked me up when I was down on myself, and early on, I was down quite a lot. When I needed someone to come along with me to a meeting, he grabbed his jacket and followed me out the door. I don't know whether, under someone else's wing, I would have gotten as far as I did.

We ended up really close. There were key points in my personal life, milestones outside of my ascension in the world of business, where he stepped in and helped me out. Without needing to be asked, he offered something of himself. We were more than just co-workers. We were friends, people that could count on one another when times were rough.

Pete Gillespie was a real mentor. He saw something deep down inside me that I'm forever grateful he took the time to get to.

GRIT AND GRIND ON THE ICE

Like most good Canadian boys, I had a dream of having a career on the ice. Every spring, I watched players circle the rink on television, holding the Stanley Cup and thought that could be me. So few actually get to, but I thought I had the stuff to be one of them. Just maybe.

My dream fell short of the National Hockey League and consequently I never got to hoist the Stanley Cup, but I ended up getting further than most kids ever do. For that I feel fortunate. After my early years playing junior hockey for the Cornwall Colts and my hometown of Kingston, Ontario for the Voyageurs, I moved up to Brown University. Then I spent a few seasons in minor league hockey in the United States, playing in cities like Bloomington, Augusta and Fayetteville before finally calling it quits.

Quitting was never in my personality. I don't know what changed in me, but looking back on that time now, I could see that I just stopped caring about the game. When I took a slap shot and missed the net, instead of gritting my teeth, determined to rip the next one, I shrugged my shoulders and continued on. Drop a pass? Same complacent feeling. What had seemed like life and death at one point simply didn't matter to me.

The passion that had driven me to this point was too far gone to get back. I knew I couldn't let my teammates down though, which I would have, had I stuck around, faking it in the faint hope of reaching a dream that I could see was rapidly disappearing. So, at the age of twenty-nine, I decided to hang up my skates for good. My hockey career, the game I had played since I was just a boy, was now over and I had to do something different.

The end of a career is a little different for every player. It is natural for most athletes to take the time necessary to reflect on their playing career when it's finally over. The goals they scored, the games they won and lost, and the players they went into battle with. All of those memories come back to you in a wave of images, in the echoed sounds of cheers and boos from the crowd. For me personally, I was fortunate enough to experience different opportunities to reflect on my career.

I always prided myself on being a hard-working, positive player. It became something like my signature quality both on the ice and in the locker room. The guy who never takes a shift off. Later in my career, I was on a team that was making a push for the playoffs. I remember that I was talking to our coach and really feeling good about our chances. I remember saying, hey, I think we're the best team out there. I think we're going to win this thing.

The coach replied, "I know we are." I snapped my head around in confusion as he looked me in the eye. He had a grin on his face that screamed, I'll take care of you boys. I won't let you lose. He saw winners in us too, and part of what made that particular team so very great was the positivity we brought to the ice. We worked and played for each other, which isn't something all teams can claim to do.

But it wasn't until I attended a wedding, years after my career ended, attended by a bunch of teammates from back in my old junior hockey Cornwall days, that I really understood the positive intangibles I brought to the rink every day. A lot of time had passed since we played together. Most everyone had moved on from pursuing their hockey dream to something else. We were just a bunch of friends, hanging around, talking about the good old days. One of the guys confided in me, as we were rubbing elbows, that if it wasn't for my influence on him in the locker room, he would have quit the game altogether.

I couldn't believe what I was hearing. "You helped me stay in the game," he went on to say. I was floored. As hard as I tried, I couldn't remember anything specific about my time with that player, but to him, our interactions stood out. It helped him stick with his dream. My career never resulted in me hoisting the Stanley Cup, but looking back now, knowing that I had a positive influence on my teammates, means a whole lot.

HELPING PEOPLE MAKE IT A GREAT DAY

When it finally came time to brand myself, I was faced with a lot of interesting choices. I had successfully applied the ideals and principles that Pete had taught me to my own business, and actually reached some acclaim. No longer lost, like I was in the very beginning, I wanted to craft a message that I could stand behind. Something that paid forward some of the powerful empathy and understanding I had been shown throughout the long path under my mentor's wing.

Then the words hit me: *Make it a great day.*

I don't remember exactly where I was when the idea struck me, but once it did, I knew that there was no going back. This was going to be who I was and the longer I sat with it, the less it felt like a sales pitch or a business email salutation. It got to the heart of a way of life that gave people control over the circumstances in their lives, and I really liked that. I was out to help make people feel awesome.

I saw that the world sorely needed positivity. I recognized that there were a lot of people who really struggled to make incremental, positive changes in their day-to-day lives. Things like getting enough sleep at night, drinking enough water, cutting loose and laughing – these are all small things that make up a vital part of our everyday wellness, and people, sadly, lose sight of doing those. In order to write the best book possible, I researched. I reached out to successful people and asked them for tips, putting that all together to deliver a healthy dose of positivity for people that needed it.

When the terrible calamity of March of 2020 hit and the entire world all but ground to a frightening halt, that unfortunate reality struck people in profound ways. More than ever before, I think, we each needed a shift in perspective. To a large extent our circumstances are under our control and a little empathy and understanding goes a long way toward bridging that gap. Life is filled with uncertainties. Pipes burst. The bus shows up late. Sometimes we wake up and, for reasons we cannot explain, our kids or spouses are angry at us.

Nothing in this life is certain except, perhaps, the idea that the empathy and understanding we show others is cyclical. I have experienced it. I was the player in the locker room, helping my teammates keep their heads up through tough times, supporting them in pursuing their dream. That all came back to me in the form of Pete Gillespie when I was lost and in need of a mentor.

I want "Make It A Great Day" to spark positivity in people. Get out there and say hello to a neighbor or a pedestrian on the street. Ask them how their day is going. Tell them they are doing a great job. Give a colleague a high five. Open a door and smile at someone.

Be a positive link in that great chain.

About Jarrett

Jarrett Robertson grew up in Kingston, Ontario, where hockey was his ultimate dream. He was extremely fortunate that his talent and hard work earned him a scholarship to the Ivy League, where he played hockey for the Brown University Bears. After graduating in 2006, before transitioning into the financial services industry, Jarrett spent two and a half years playing semi-pro hockey throughout the U.S., trying to make the big leagues.

Shortly after his career in hockey was over, and he 'hung up his skates', he was lucky to connect with an old friend, who helped get him involved in the fitness industry. It was from there that he learned so much about overall health and well-being, and it's those things that have been paramount in his success, both personally and professionally.

Jarrett is proud to hold the Certified Financial Planner designation (CFP®), the most widely recognized financial planning designation in Canada and worldwide. The Certified Financial Planner® designation provides assurance to Canadians that the design of their financial future rests with a professional who will put their clients' interests ahead of their own.

CFP professionals demonstrate the knowledge, skills, experience and ethics to examine their clients' entire financial picture, at the highest level of complexity required of the profession, and work with their clients to build a financial plan so that they can Live Life Confidently™. Jarrett is an Executive Circle member of the Financial Psychology Institute, a multi-published author, and a Psychology of Financial Planning Specialist™.

Jarrett has found that, like anything in life, you can research more, dig deeper, go further, climb higher, etc., but what he has learned is that it's the little things that we can do every day that will actually help us get started—the prologue—if you will. People do not plan on failing, but people do fail to plan.

He helps to motivate people by always looking for a solution on how to achieve success or solve a problem, and by always being positive. Currently Jarrett lives in the Greater Toronto Area with his wife, Lacey, and their two sons, Hudson and Benton.

Not every day is easy but every day my reasons are my wife and my two boys.
Life is not too short; life is extremely valuable.
~ JR

CHAPTER 19

THE POWER OF THREE

BY NEAL TURNER

PAST. PRESENT. FUTURE.

INCEPTION. LIFE. DEATH.

MIND. BODY. BREATH.

Three is a powerful, sacred number. That's why this isn't my story alone—or Meisha's story—but the story of two people coming together.

- How a unified vision can create something positive.

- How the profound beauty of collaboration creates a whole that's bigger than the individual parts.

Empathy is understanding, but it's also a compassionate act that starts and ends with self. Being empathetic to self with calm, simple practices creates a naturally compounding effect of honesty of effort. In everything, the most profound power of three comes back to the same triad: *Me. You. Us.*

———≈———

The Marbella Gymnastics Club started as our gift to each other. With our backgrounds in sport, a nonprofit organization offering artistic gymnastics was a natural choice.

I'm a martial arts student and instructor, personal trainer, breathwork practitioner, and mentor. I focus on holistic practices and 'sounding out sessions,' helping people talk through and logically process a problem by empowering them with simple tools and skills. Meisha is a former UK elite-level gymnast and autograss champion with ten years of coaching all ages in gymnastics, gymnastics-based dance, and CrossFit.

Meisha and I devised the dream of this club while working, living, and meditating in the home we spent two years building together. Three meters wide throughout. Twenty-eight degree angles. Expansive windows pouring natural light into the space. Skylights tracking celestial bodies—sun, moon, stars—as they arc across the night sky. Every architectural touch is a nod to the stoicism we both practice.

Once the idea took root, we sat in our home and wrote down our plan. We researched. We looked into laws and regulations. We watched this shared idea take physical shape, transforming from thought to ink to reality.

We wanted to experience new cultures, foods, and languages, so we sought a location outside England. Eventually we landed in Spain. We made the move in 2013. After arriving, we stumbled through language barriers and bureaucratic red tape, approaching local schools and offering our gymnastics services.

The children, parents, and community loved it. We gained enough traction to move into our own facility. With continued success, we soon moved into an even bigger location.

Offering classes to boys and girls five years and older, we were equipped to an Olympic level with AirTracks, uneven bars, balance beams, vaulting tables, trampolines, and freestyle blocks.

The dedicated facility sat in the middle of Andalusia, a sprawling autonomous region on Spain's southern coast. It's a fairytale land with an idyllic microclimate and hills, rivers, and farmland dotting the landscape. It's also a place of extremes. Wealth and poverty coexisting in the same town—and our club in the middle of it all.

Again, the power of three was there. Two ends of the economic spectrum and us, a balancing center of equanimity and neutrality. We were a place of welcome, calm, and discipline. Anyone who wanted lessons received them at the same price, regardless of social standing or economic position.

In those early days, neighbors warned us in a broken mix of Spanish and English about break-ins. "Beware of your security," they repeatedly said. I scrawled a note and attached it to our door. It read:

If you want to break in, we'll teach you for free.

Some local children soon took our offer. We did our sessions, gifting them with structured movement, foundational concepts of breath and calming, and focused discipline. We saw those children often, zooming the streets on their rusted bikes. After our sessions, they always offered shy, respectful waves and a friendly chorus of "Hola!"

Meeting intended hostility with proactive kindness, that understanding forged a meaningful bond with the community.

———≈———

MIND

I left school at fifteen. I knew I learned better with my hands, and I soon found myself on building sites. As the damp and chill of winter set in, I worked construction jobs around England's hub of red top newspapers. Out in the cold, a child among a crew of men, I realized my mistake. I hadn't been patient enough. I always learn the hard way, but I do learn.

When I began martial arts, I took those hard-earned lessons of patience and perspective. In the dojo, one credo rules. No shoes. No egos. When entering a training space, those are surrendered. From the newest students to black belts—people with years of practiced dedication—everyone has this shared mentality.

Today, I take that mindset into any space. In the dojo. With my students. In every fraught meeting I had with local Spanish officials to secure our business licenses.

We were extremely selective about the club's instructors. Every coach had extensive qualifications from the United Kingdom, Spain, and the United States. They were trained and experienced in gymnastics, trampolining, calisthenics, speed, agility, and quickness (SAQ), and strength and conditioning. They were first aiders, held child protections qualifications, and had passed all disclosure and barring service checks.

Beyond that, though, every coach had to embrace this idea. No shoes. No egos. It applied to me, Meisha, our students, parents, and the other instructors. We only invested in those who exhibited the physical, mental, and emotional principles we wanted to instill through gymnastics. Every day, we thoroughly cleaned the club. Throughout every lesson, we sustained our bodies with water. Every coach had the correct credentials and training.

We ran through these mental checklists. We leaned on the power of three:

Plan. Prepare. Practice.

----~----

BODY

Structured for optimal performance, we began with warm-ups, including greetings, mobility, and flexibility work. We also spent this time on personal connections and buddying up new, shy, or nervous kids with more seasoned gymnasts in the club.

We then moved into apparatus work, guiding each student to their personal goals. (Class sizes were limited to ensure every gymnast could reach those goals, including participation in grades, exams, competitions, and displays.) We finished with "the accumulation of potential"—an opportunity for each child, no matter the level, to showcase the skills they'd learned in the session.

Through gymnastics, we explored and pushed the potential of the human body and performance. Gymnastics is a dynamic exploration of rotation and gravity. It requires physical core control, which becomes a foundation for mental control.

Just as an architectural feat requires blueprints, executing complicated gymnastics series requires a solid foundation. Of mind, body, and breath.

This idea became critical for me during our transition to Spain. One of the most difficult periods of my life, I continually relied on my physical and mental foundations to persevere. It started when I broke my back in an unexpected accident in the garden. With tremendous effort, I worked through that physical and mental pain.

My initial time in Spain was largely spent recovering. After six months, my body was just beginning to heal. Then, after a few weeks of hosting classes, I fell ill with viral meningitis. My brain swelled and pushed against my skull, sending me into a partially conscious coma for seven days and nights.

By my bedside in a land that wasn't yet home, Meisha watched me battle. Incoherent. Disoriented. Exhausted. I was fueled by morphine for the pain and caffeine to help replace the infected fluids in my spine and brain. Meisha tried to make sense of the array of tubes and machines as my caffeine-laced brain raced with irrational thoughts.

Throughout the ordeal, my team of doctors and nurses offered brilliant care and amazing support. They welcomed Meisha every visiting time with warm, encouraging smiles. Despite the language barrier, they made sure Meisha understood every treatment and medication I was receiving.

We'll never forget their kindness and adept skill. After I discharged myself on day eight, I spent a year relearning the mechanics of my body and mind. I couldn't walk or speak. I had completely lost my Spanish and most of my English.

When faced with trauma, we all have a choice: let the darkness consume us or grow toward the light. We both chose growth. The power of three directed our lives again. This time it was: determination, grit, and stubbornness.

My intense medical rehabilitation included mapping my genome. Numerous medications continually replaced my spinal fluid and fought infection. The majority of my rehabilitation was spent in bed. Exhausted and anxious, I applied what energy I had to breathing exercises, gentle yoga, listening to calm music, and journaling. Page after page of processing research, clarifying data, and summarizing the skills, tools, and methods to promote calm.

I was continually empowered by the knowledge I could execute change and promote progress using just the tools I already possessed—mind, body, breath.

Once I regained enough energy, Meisha drove me to the beach so I could walk in the sand and sea. I juggled to rediscover my motor skills and lay on my back just beyond the waves. Ears below water. Body suspended. Eyes closed. I listened to the waves come in and out and the soft rumble of pebbles against the seabed. I meditated and breathed to these sounds as the saltwater lapped against my body. In and out with the waves. Pause with the pebbles. In. Out. Pause.

With science, rest, Meisha's unwavering support, consistent effort, and calm practices, I was able to will my body back into mobility and speech. Again and again, I drew on my well of training and foundations to move incrementally forward.

As a martial arts student and instructor, I teach people how to tap into the potential of their bodies. How to be hunched like a lion or coiled like a snake—not in tense anxiety but from a position of readiness. An ability to launch into a sprint when needed.

But the physical component of the art—performing that kick or neutralizing someone with that elbow—is only one piece of the discipline. Most of what I teach is knowing how to run. Assessing where the exit is. Honing that ability to sense trouble and proactively not get involved.

That's the foundation.

To use the physical skills responsibly, a student must enter into the sport with humility, understanding, and empathy. I used that combination of physical and mental training to piece together my recovery. To turn one faltering step into two. To grasp that word and the next until I was again stringing thoughts into sentences. Translating what was in my mind and giving it space in the physical world. I was continually reminded of what's possible with progressive discipline.

In Marbella Gymnastics Club, everything was done step by step. The skills were even broken down into visual guides on the wall. Kids could see how each logical, progressive step got them closer to that end goal. The cartwheel. The backflip. The double back tucked salto.

Whatever the goal, we broke down the movement into pieces, we practiced, and then we put all those components together.

BREATH

Before any tumbling sequence, students were invited to take three calming breaths. Everything has energy potential. Anxiety brings frenetic, overanalytical energy. Meditation and focus bring nonjudgmental, accountable honesty of effort and clarity.

Using just your breath, you can manifest peace and tranquility. Mindful breathing brings everything into balance. Calm, slow breaths signal to our brains everything's OK, triggering a relaxation response.

Breath became our centering tool when COVID hit. As a nonprofit charity, we relied on class fees. With the first lockdown, those funds stopped. Without governmental support, we made the difficult decision to close the club and move back to England. After everything we'd worked to build, we were profoundly disappointed—for the children, the staff, and ourselves.

During the second lockdown, we began studying anxiety. We felt the disconnection of COVID, as well as the stress of losing our business. We saw anxiety mounting around us, especially in children. Pivoting our business model and employing some creativity, we began advertising our globally-recognized and applauded teaching methods for Zoom based gymnastics lessons.

One of the first bookings came from a mother across the globe. She wanted a female coach to teach her and her daughters while still complying with her country's rules and respecting her religion. We were delighted to accept.

Inhale. Exhale. Pause.

By taking a breath and allowing ourselves that pause, we had time to view the problem more creatively. By being empathetic to ourselves and our potential students, we fostered a connection in a time of deep isolation. We connected with a family thousands of miles away, even while living under strict lockdown. We'll never forget the smiles of those kids and their mother.

———————≈———————

UNITY

Power comes from collaboration, connection, and understanding. When entities work together, that unity elevates each part of the whole.

Mind. Body. Breath.

This philosophy teaches practices that empower and enable empathy. Empathy is an act. It can be carried out. It can be practiced—for self and others.

Just as journaling is an emotional intelligence tool promoting self-awareness and exploration in a nonjudgmental space, so too is sitting comfortably in a calm position with calm breath.

Calm-ing.

Breath in. Breath out. Pause.

As logical beings, humans look to impose judgment, order, and understanding. By giving yourself the space to sit comfortably, your mind, body, and breath can work in unity.

Meditation is a superpower, calming the mind so it can stay undivided and on task. Suddenly the relationships between the gifts bestowed upon us become evident. This mindful state helps us maintain a calm, curious nature and proceed from a non-judgmental place. Our club was that safe space.

On any given day, children from around the globe came. Walking through the door, I always heard a handful of different languages. Spanish. Swedish. Russian. English. Above the jumble of excited chatter, one word rang out.

"Nice."

The children all gravitated toward this word. It became a touchstone of understanding and connection. They created their own adaptive communication. When someone landed a difficult sequence, 'nice' was a groundswell of support from their fellow gymnasts. When someone mastered a move, 'nice' was a triumphant self-affirmation.

The club was an eclectic mix of kids. Quiet introverts and outgoing extroverts. The children, though, didn't see those differences as divisive. Leading with understanding, they helped each other. Extroverts displayed the benefits of outward-facing energy. Introverts taught the virtue of reflection and self-examination.

In our club hung a banner reading, Those who say they can and those who say they can't are both usually right. We displayed this quote as a reminder of our potential, positivity, confidence, and commitment. We'd often hear kids telling fellow classmates, "Go read the sign. You can do it. You've got this!"

Meisha and I have dedicated our lives to human performance and making a positive impact on individuals, but true lessons of empathy, congruence, and community happened organically and spontaneously every day among our students.

In our endeavors and all around, the power of three is there –

CONNECTION. UNDERSTANDING. EMPATHY.

Namaste!

About Neal

Neal Turner's career is dedicated to enhancing human performance and personal growth. He has transformed countless lives by providing them with the tools, skills and methods to maximize their potential and realize their aspirations.

Neal is a committed Martial Arts Student and Instructor focused on the core principles of Respect, Dedication and Mindfulness.

Neal played a pivotal role in shaping the careers of two promising Mixed Martial Artists. Recognizing the immense potential of MMA early on, Neal coached and mentored these athletes through the intricate world of the sport, elevating them to professional recognition. Their journey, marked by Neal's guidance, not only showcased their talent, but also solidified his reputation as a mentor and coach in human performance.

Neal is instrumental in mentoring Professional Motorbike Riders, providing technical skills and holistic practices that encompass race craft on and off the bike, psychology of competition and mental resilience. With Neal's guidance, these riders not only secure victories but are consistently establishing themselves as dominant forces in the world of motorbike racing.

Neals coaching techniques are renowned for being logical, attainable and usable, producing desirable results that are congruent with the individual. His impact extends across a diverse range of industries and demographics, and he has successfully coached CEOs, Professional Athletes, Leaders, Parents and Children on how implementing simple daily practices – 5 mins Yoga, 5 mins Affirmations, 5 mins Contemplation – are the foundation to cultivate healthy habits and achieve success.

In addition to his work in performance coaching, Neal has shown a commitment to community and inclusivity. He founded the Marbella Gymnastics Club, a non-profit organization, promoting physical fitness, discipline and teamwork among youth in underprivileged areas. In recognition of his dedication to creating a positive and nurturing environment, Neal was granted two Business Licenses by the Spanish Government in 2019.

Currently, Neal, along with his fiancée, Meisha, is co-authoring a workbook for children that promotes calm and supports children's mental well-being. The workbook provides fun and engaging methods to help children create calm, navigate daily challenges and promote emotional resilience and overall mental stability.

This book, alongside Boom Boom Gymnastics which Neal is currently setting up, puts him at the forefront of grass roots in Essex, his 3-year goal after the forced relocation from Spain.

Neal Turner's commitment to achieving results is complimented by his unwavering devotion to personal and professional growth. He actively participates in ongoing education, masterclasses and courses to enhance his skills and expand his knowledge, ensuring he remains at the forefront of his field.

Collaboration and community building are fundamental to Neal's approach. He frequently seeks opportunities to connect with professionals from diverse industries, recognizing the value of interdisciplinary cooperation in unlocking human potential. His ability to foster collaboration and bring individuals together is instrumental to his success.

To learn more about Neal, visit:

- www.theartofcalming.org
- www.mindbodybreathcoaching.com

CHAPTER 20

THE HUMAN SIDE OF DATA

BY ANDREW C. BAUTA

When Mike found his son, he was across county lines in a homeless shelter.

Mike was expelled in the ninth grade and never went back to school. He became a father as a teenager. His son's equally young mother struggled with substance abuse and poverty. When she kidnapped his son, Mike leveraged the newest tool at his disposal. Data!

Computers, the internet, and networking technology were just becoming mainstream. But Mike had already taught himself the ins and outs of these systems—especially how to get into unsecured systems and get out valuable data. Text messages. Social media posts. Geolocation data. From this information, he built a timeline and a compelling narrative around the kidnapping. Eventually, that narrative convinced a judge to grant him full custody of his son.

Most people don't think about the data their lives generate. But Mike leveraged that data to tell a living story that saved his son's life. Mike didn't have the terminology then, but he had found his first Black Swan – not shared willingly during a negotiation, but discovered in the data everyone unknowingly creates.

FROM PAYPAL SCHEMES TO
THE U.S. ATTORNEY'S OFFICE

Mike later became my business partner, my brother-in-law, and our company's founder. But his earlier life had a profound impact on him and the company we now run together.

Mike was raised in an unorthodox home. The children of a successful software developer, he and his two sisters had no active parenting or boundaries. They lived in a multimillion-dollar home, and whatever they wanted, they got. Mike was only five when he received his first computer, but he plunged into the nascent tech landscape with uncanny intuition.

When his parents suddenly divorced, that privileged life dwindled. The kids jumped between homes and parents. They moved several times each year—and not always together. A mansion became a townhouse, which became a friend's couch.

Looking to bring money back into his life, Mike began hacking at eleven. Selling and trading digital data, Mike figured out how to siphon funds and generate sales from unsecured gaming accounts and payment portals.

Watching all this happen, Mike's sister eventually said he had two choices: continue and end up in jail or get a real job. She pulled some strings, and on his eighteenth birthday, Mike became an entry-level scanner with the US Attorney's Office. Within two years, he leveraged his unique experience and self-taught technical insight to become accepted as the then-youngest special agent with the Department of Defense.

Bypassing degrees and certifications, Mike used his hands-on, real-world expertise to augment investigations by the Secret Service, Department of Defense, and other agencies. This included writing evidence-sorting code in the *US v. AEY, Inc.* investigation (later dramatized in the 2016 film *War Dogs*).

As his family grew, Mike eventually entered the private sector. He worked for a large law firm for several years before starting his own digital forensics consulting firm, Lawgical Insight.

AN UNDIAGNOSED LIFE

For most of my life, I lived with undiagnosed Autism Spectrum Disorder ("autism"). I was lucky to be born with high general intelligence. So, despite my undiagnosed autism, I made it through school. I earned an undergraduate degree in aerospace engineering and completed law school. I even had some workplace success, completing a judicial clerkship for a federal judge and working as a litigator in a Big Law firm.

I routinely used my intellect to suppress autistic behaviors and compensate for social difficulties, including sensory overload. This is called masking. It helped, but I was rapidly draining my intellectual and emotional resources. Conversation by conversation. Assignment by assignment.

Like all autistics, I struggled with face-to-face interactions, especially in professional settings. I had difficulty reading people correctly—and understanding why I wasn't being read correctly. This is called the double empathy problem. I repeatedly heard the same feedback while in high-stakes, high-stress litigation. Your work is great. We just don't know if you're a good fit.

Then I was in a serious car accident. The injuries made it harder to sit and think for long stretches. I realized I had to rethink my career. I tried several other avenues, including high-end car sales and an executive position with a medical supply company. This executive position was going well enough...until the pandemic hit. Emergency healthcare eclipsed elective healthcare. Corporate revenue plummeted by over 50 percent, almost overnight. I was a new, big-ticket hire, and I was out.

This coincided with Mike starting Lawgical Insight. I joined Mike, and we discovered we had complementary strengths. Mike was good at people and computers. I was good at strategy and sales. Shortly after I came on board, we quadrupled our caseload.

KNOW THYSELF, A TACTICAL EMPATHY TALE

In law school, I met Mike's sister, Christine. Early in our marriage, Christine became the first person to suggest I was autistic. Although prior girlfriends certainly had suggested I go to therapy. (Did that joke land? That was an autistic question. And that was an autistic comment.)

A formal diagnosis gave me clarity. I could finally articulate the delta between me and seemingly everyone else. But that was only half the battle. I still had to determine how to close that delta without being overwhelmed. I had to address the double empathy problem.

It's a deep misconception that autistics lack empathy. They just display poor real-time empathy—especially face-to-face with non-autistics. So, what happens during these face-to-face meetings? Autistics follow the Golden Rule, treating others the way autistics want to be treated. But that's a problem when you aren't like everyone else.

In part, autistics are different because sensory inputs (sounds, unexpected visuals, textures) overwhelm them. When I'm trying to avoid a headache from the car alarm outside, it's hard to understand that you're asking about my weekend plans because you want to share yours. I'll just answer your question and move on.

When I read *Never Split the Difference*, it immediately made sense. It formalized the autistic masking I was managing in the background. Chris Voss's Tactical Empathy provided a framework for three important tasks:

First – recognizing which interactions called for purposeful, attentive empathy: all of them. This is Voss's Platinum Rule: treat others the way they *need* to be treated.

Second – developing a consistent method of applying empathy: rules for socializing with non-autistics. For example, I stopped waiting for my turn to talk and then saying something I hoped was relevant. Instead, I mirror until someone stops offering new information or asks me a question.

Third – identifying goal posts to mark social transitions. When the next question isn't obvious, I can craft calibrated questions, labels, or even an accusation audit. This moves us toward a 'That's right' or a Black Swan, which is when I know you feel understood.

Applying Voss's framework means I don't have to solve social interactions in real time. I can be proactive and productive about expected situations. And then fall back on Tactical Empathy for the unexpected.

WE ARE *LAWGICAL INSIGHT*

This is great news because a significant part of what Mike and I do is either interacting socially with stakeholders or engaging in social engineering.

Lawgical Insight is a digital evidence consultancy. We help law firms, companies, and individuals find, secure, and review data to build persuasive stories ('eDiscovery'). It's usually done during a lawsuit, government or corporate investigation, or cyber-crime response. Our cases have ranged from a billion-dollar Mafia-run Ponzi scheme to murder-for-hire plots to celebrity cyber-stalking and -impersonation.

Whether we're finding evidence or manipulating technology to access it, our job requires that we understand how others think and feel. Litigation was once about finding the right person or asking the right question. Now, it's about finding the right email or asking for the right call record.

Today, criminals can organize a conspiracy in a video game chat room. Everyone uses a personal smartphone for work. Even a decent-sized company can generate over 50,000 emails daily. And that was all before generative artificial intelligence ('gen-AI').

So, how does anyone find that right email? Or ask for that right call record? Then how do you turn the right emails or call records into a story? How do you convince a jury (in just a few minutes) to believe your claims or persuade an insurance company to offer a settlement? It's a lot, but we can help!

Given Mike's experience with his son, he's keenly aware of the power behind building stories from data. And given my autism, I understand that influence comes from leading people the way they need to be led.

GETTING TO TRUST

Lawgical Insight is in an unusual position. We act as the bridge between governance, people, and digital evidence. So, the biggest demands on our leadership are with external stakeholders, not internal employees.

Trust is central to everything we do. We need trust from a variety of stakeholders—often with competing interests. We need trust from our clients, witnesses, and the judges and juries who rely on our expert opinions and trial narratives. We even need trust from adverse parties who would question our work.

We often ask clients and witnesses to divulge sensitive information during stressful, frightening times. Maybe they're worried about going to jail, losing their company, or destroying their reputation. But if gaining stakeholder trust is hard on a good day, how do we gain it on their worst day?

Trust only comes when we approach stakeholders with genuine empathy. They must believe in our technical expertise and trust our leadership. Voss helped us recognize that every engagement—every stakeholder interview or closing argument at trial—can be framed as a negotiation.

Using empathy, we can get positive answers to the questions we need to deliver results.

Will you trust us:

- With your communications, trade secrets, and web search history?
- To tell a good story well, whether to a jury or opposing party?
- To only disclose the necessary parts of your story?

In these negotiations, we have almost no bargaining power. We can't pay witnesses to divulge if they offloaded company data to private servers. We can't fire CEOs if they don't relinquish personal iPhones.

All we can offer is empathetic leadership.

TACTICAL EMPATHY AT THE SPEED OF BUSINESS

Join me on a witness interview. We have about ten minutes with James. We need to know everywhere he might have Corporation's data. We need every device or account, business or personal, that might have evidence related to the government's investigation. He's withholding information. We suspect James committed a crime. The lawyer is our client, Corporation pays our bills, and James works for Corporation.

Oh, great. The lawyer just took four of our minutes explaining everything. We're up.

Accusation audit. We got a 'no' and some buy-in. Nice. Question, question, question. Oops. Those weren't calibrated. Calibrated question. Better answer. There's a Black Swan in here somewhere. We just need...

And we're out of time.

That's how Lawgical Insight ran for a while. After reading Voss's book, we immediately understood Tactical Empathy's value, but his method is an iceberg. Above the surface, it's deceptively simple. But under the surface, the application is a huge challenge—especially if you want consistent application, across a team, at the speed of business.

We learned to employ Tactical Empathy at the speed of our business by leveraging gen-AI.

We use gen-AI to analyze data, predict stakeholder perspectives, and formulate calibrated questions and labels. We feed the gen-AI case-specific information and documents. Then we use the gen-AI's responses to develop precise, strategic accusation audits. We even generate bespoke negotiation one-sheets for each stakeholder. You can perform even better with gen-AI plug-ins or skills. These limit gen-AIs to responding based on a specific document or data source (e.g., NASA database or published caselaw).

We'll skip over how gen-AI works. For now, the important thing is your team's use of prompts. Below is our system for prompting gen-AIs for labels, calibrated questions, accusation audits, and negotiation one-sheets. For this system, run through the steps for each stakeholder's perspective.

In a direct negotiation, you might only have one stakeholder (your opposing party). In other negotiations, you might have several.

Prepare Your Gen-AI's Brief

If you don't have any documents relevant to the negotiation, skip to step 4.

1) Upload relevant documents to the gen-AI (emails, contracts, proposals). Choose the most important ones.
2) Ask the gen-AI to summarize these documents.
3) Copy the summaries into a document called 'Brief.'
4) Start the Brief with the following details:
    a) Your stake –
       e.g., I'm trying to close a deal on a sales contract for Y item.
    b) Other stakeholders –
       e.g., There are two competing offers from Party 1 and Party 2, and Client will make the final decision.
    c) Key facts –
       e.g., The contract must close by Date. The other offers are unknown.
    d) Key issues or problems –
       e.g., I'm the smallest vendor. I have more relevant expertise, but I cannot get face time with Client. Client's Agent doesn't like me.
    e) Desired outcome –
       e.g., I want Client to accept my bid or agree to meet with me before deciding.
    f) Relevant context from documents (if applicable) –
       e.g., Here are summaries of three documents relevant to the above negotiation.

Your summaries from step 3 follow.

Brief Goes In; Tactical Empathy Comes Out

1) Prompt the gen-AI with an appropriate voice. For example:

   a) Take the position of a business owner who won't pay for my services.

   b) Act like an expert in human resources compliance.

   c) Pretend you're expert negotiator Chris Voss.

2) Tell the gen-AI you'll give it context for a negotiation. Copy and paste your Brief as a prompt.

3) Give the gen-AI a task or instruction. For example:

   a) Think deeply about preparing a negotiation one-sheet in the style of *Never Split the Difference*. Make one for the above scenario.

   b) Think critically about how a neutral jury would react to the scenario above. Prepare five accusation audits in the style of *Never Split the Difference*.

   c) Identify the contractual terms you think are unfair.

   d) Generate ten Voss-style calibrated questions to ask you.

4) Since the gen-AI can assume your stakeholder's perspective, test your labels, calibrated questions, and accusation audits as new prompts. See how it responds.

5) If the response isn't quite right, prompt the gen-AI to change its focus or tone –
   e.g., this accusation audit has useful content, but try again with a casual tone.

Note: Ensure the task matches the voice. Don't ask the HR expert for a one-sheet.

AI helps us work faster, gives us insight into different perspectives, and offers repeatable frameworks and processes at scale—especially when you use a shared database to capture institutional knowledge about your prompts, gen-AI responses, and relevant use cases.

The emerging adage is that gen-AI won't replace you but someone who uses gen-AI will. For Mike and me, gen-AI has been the two millimeter shift that makes Lawgical Insight just a little better—and more empathetic—than our competitors.

About Andrew

Andrew C. Bauta is a lawyer and engineer, with over a decade of experience in business, litigation, and technology integration. He is a Principal at Lawgical Insight. He has worked in the following industries: aerospace; automotive; education; film production; finance; firearms; and healthcare.

Andrew has handled legal matters in the following practice areas: bankruptcy, business litigation, contract negotiation, employment, governmental compliance, healthcare, intellectual property and entertainment, internal investigations, and international law. This breadth of experience allows him to slip into roles, communicate effectively, and ideate in a variety of industries and at various levels of a business or transaction.

Andrew's bachelor's in aerospace engineering is from Georgia Tech, from which he graduated with honors. His J.D. is from the University of Florida. He is barred, and admitted to federal courts, in Florida. He honed his legal acumen as Judicial Law Clerk to the Hon. James Lawrence King, United States District Court, Southern District of Florida.

Lawgical Insight is a consulting firm, operating at the nexus of law and technology. It specializes in digital investigations, cyber-crime response, eDiscovery management, trial preparation, and gen-AI integration. From courtrooms to boardrooms, Lawgical Insight leads clients as they transform their data into cogent legal narratives.

Lawgical Insight was founded by Michael W. Russo and is helmed by Andrew. Michael is a Certified e-Discovery Specialist (CEDS) with over fifteen years of experience in digital forensics, eDiscovery, and litigation support. His government career spans four offices of the United States Attorney's Office. His criminal and forensic experience includes investigations into – and augmenting defense of – financial crimes, internet crimes, white collar crimes, terrorism, and other major crimes. His civil experience includes prosecution and defense of cases involving insurance, health care, class actions and mass claims, securities, and complex commercial litigation. No matter the issue, Michael has seen it, or its like, before.

Lawgical Insight has served federal enforcement agencies, Am Law 100 firms, Fortune 500 companies, litigation boutique firms, and individual celebrities. Lawgical Insight's people have a laundry list of certifications--a testament to their technical prowess. But the important problems can't be found in textbooks or on standardized tests. So Lawgical Insight's true distinction lies in its avant-garde problem-solving abilities, with solutions often forged in real-time. Whether gleaning insights from an intense GitHub discussion, engaging in high-octane Discord debates, or pouring over cutting-edge research on arxiv.org, Lawgical Insight's people are always on the pulse.

Lawgical Insight's work covers the gamut of digital forensics, eDiscovery, and technology integration. From hardware management to network infrastructure and software development; from scope-of-discovery issues to production compliance; and from active intrusion response to employee education. Lawgical Insight has saved clients millions of dollars by auditing existing e-Discovery environments – correcting system and workflow inefficiencies, ensuring governance and compliance, preventing inadvertent production of sensitive materials, and creating custom solutions to automate manual efforts.

Lawgical Insight can help with:

- End-to-end eDiscovery lifecycle.
- Network intrusion response.
- Cyber-stalking, -impersonation, or -harassment.
- Gen-AI productivity integration, including personnel training.
- Trial consulting and support.

Learn more, worry less; connect with *lawgicalinsight.com.*

CHAPTER 21

FROM BATTLEFIELDS TO BULL MARKETS: PRESERVING DEMOCRACY THROUGH EMPATHY

BY DAMON PAULL

"Life is a competitive endeavor. You don't get a trophy in the real world just for showing up. You get it for achieving true excellence.
But individual excellence is not enough.
We also need to be the best team players we can be."
~ Quote conveyed to me by General David Petraeus, US Army (Ret.);
former Commander of the Surge in Iraq, US Central Command, and
NATO/US Forces in Afghanistan; former Director of the CIA.

[Details withheld to protect national security.]

Belgium, past 0600. Darkness engulfed me, and the air felt thick under the tarp. I jostled wildly with every bump as the US Marine vehicle pulled up to the housing gate. I silently prayed there would not be a vehicle inspection where I would be discovered.

My creativity for getting past the Master Sergeant's 0600 curfew was forever evolving in my young Marine mind. A combination of immaturity and never being one to color inside the lines meant I had missed one too many military curfews already. I could not afford to be caught.

My best option this time was disguising myself under a decaying tarp and deploying some cover and concealment skills learned from my previous California infantry unit.

Thankfully, we were not selected for a random vehicle inspection, and Master Sergeant was none the wiser. Decades later, I am still grateful to that Belgian driver who took on the additional risk of ferrying me back to safety...more than once.

Why the tarp and subterfuge? At the time, this Master Sergeant kept young men like me in line by being fanatical about rules and micromanaging every movement. He routinely stationed himself several blocks away from the Marine house with binoculars to see who arrived home late or which girlfriends stayed past Cinderella curfew. He tracked the movements of his own team so intently he often seemed like a one-man countersurveillance team.

In all seriousness, I understood the importance of random reaction drills and keeping the spear razor sharp. We were there to protect US interests at NATO headquarters and other vital US government assets. That was not a job to be taken lightly.

However, the amount of control this leader exerted over our lives was stifling. There was no trust. No understanding. No respect. No empathy.

HOW BAD LEADERSHIP CHANGED MY LIFE

I grew up in the Virginia Beach and Kansas City areas. After graduating from high school, I dove into the extraordinary record of legendary veteran 'White Feather', Carlos Hathcock, in *Marine Sniper: 93 Confirmed Kills*.

My dad was a US Navy reservist stationed at Little Creek, Virginia, where the elite maritime force of the US Navy SEALS is stationed. I begged my dad to call in some favors so I could actually talk to Carlos.

When we met, Carlos was extremely gracious, and he even signed my book. I was sold. Shortly after, I traded my Kid Rock style for a new signature high-and-tight haircut and a fledgling Marine contract.

When I first signed up for the US Marines, I had every intention of doing twenty-plus years of active duty and then retiring on a beach where I could drink Mai Tais. With one poor leader, that dream was burned to the ground. With stern conviction, I vowed to never again allow another person to have as much control over my everyday life as this Master Sergeant.

Unempathetic leadership changed the entire trajectory of my life. However, it also put me on a path where I experienced amazing, humbling, and incredibly inspiring leadership. After completing tours in Brussels, Istanbul, and Cairo, I separated from the US Marine Corps and chose the more ambiguous road of a defense contractor. My new home became the US Embassy in Kabul, and my mission was on the team that protected Ambassador Zalmay Khalilzad. The leadership I experienced there was the polar opposite of that Master Sergeant.

Every day, I was surrounded by the perfect blend of US Special Operations Command (SOCOM) and other veterans, and Ambassador Khalilzad was truly an inspirational leader. Not only did he wholly understand Afghan culture and the perilous challenges of building a better post-Taliban Afghanistan, but he consistently greeted his security personnel by name and visited us often. He showed us that he appreciated the grave risks our teams were taking, and he genuinely expressed interest in our lives.

Due to his skill, understanding of the local population, and respect for his personnel, our teams were exceptionally dedicated to this mission. We accepted that returning home was never guaranteed. In the end, because of this inspirational leadership, I happily volunteered to support other teams and assist in other missions. (Looking back, I acknowledge my risk management compass was a bit different back then!)

Later, I worked for a counternarcotics team under the US Department of State during the post-Taliban heroin boom. Several of the former Special Forces leaders were also shining examples of selfless service and authentic leadership.

As life marched onward, I continued to experience shades of good and bad leadership. I can say with certainty that empathetic leaders value, listen to, and respect their people, and that motivates them to work with much more intensity. A team is more successful when they know their leader sincerely works for them.

Immersing into full civilian life, I found myself managing a union team at the world's largest auto manufacturer, General Motors. My team built Chevy engines, and I have loved Chevy horses since my impressionable teenage years.

This was, however, one of the most challenging leadership roles because there is a polarizing dynamic between the management team and the union team. Management did not want to concede a millimeter to the union, and the union was not giving a nanometer without a concession. In stark contrast to the military mantra 'one team, one fight,' I had to delicately walk the razor-thin tightrope of those politics, being the lightning rod between the opposing entities.

Still not sold on the power of empathy? One empathic manufacturing leader (with a son in SOCOM) motivated me so much that I would routinely work most holidays and Saturdays. I even stayed into the next shift to assist in operations management, all on salary pay.

My real passion, though, is clearly finance. It has been a simmering spark inside me ever since reading *Play Money*, by Laura Pedersen, as a teenager. Today, I love working for an independent financial firm, where I am able to offer custom solutions to accommodate my client's financial needs, wants, and goals.

At every turn in my varied career, from the sandpits to the production floor to managed portfolios, I have experienced or demonstrated leadership. Through those firsthand experiences, I have seen what leadership tactics work...and what causes failure and hostile work environments.

EMPATHETIC VS. TOXIC LEADERSHIP

Good or lackluster, every leader I have worked with has taught me invaluable lessons. By studying how they operate, I discovered why it is so important (and how it is possible) for leaders to remain human—even in the most stressful, dire situations.

Empathy defines effective leaders and poor leaders. All the positive, inspiring leaders I have ever known have revealed that empathy is not one solitary item or act. It is a consistent, multifaceted accumulation of actions.

Traits of Empathetic Leaders

- Taking care of your people and understanding them, even when they come from different backgrounds.

- Actively listening to your team and showing genuine, authentic interest in their lives. You never know a person's story unless you inquire. Your employee may be raising a child who is a first-generation college graduate. The security personnel may save your life after an explosion or outbreak of gunfire.

- Inspiring motivation. In today's climate, loyalty is transitory. With improved pay, transparency and more robust networks, workers are more inclined to switch careers and companies.

- Only asking your team to do things you would do or have done.

- Seeing everyone as equally worthy of respect.

- Taking every opportunity to give your team members credit, especially in meetings with upper-level management where those team members are absent.

- Trusting the individuals in your team.

- Empowering individuals by delegating tasks to team members with the precise skillset.

- Ownership of the team's performance.

Traits of Toxic Leaders

- Treating workers like robots.

- Lack of discretion. Empathetic leaders do not publicly embarrass their people in front of peers.

- Making assumptions about team members.

- Churning and burning their teams and blaming generational workforce ethics. If turnover is continuously high, is the root cause Human Resources, your workers, or you?

- Displaying post-promotion snobbishness.
- Taking undue credit. Your team helped you beat that Key Performance Indicator.
- Micromanaging because of lack of trust. Define your expectations, monitor periodically.
- Being a perpetual 'yes' person to upper management. Know the capability limits of your team.

LEADERSHIP LESSONS FROM THE SANDPITS

In an active war zone, everyone on a team must come together. All those ludicrous surface-level differences (red versus blue ideology, skin color, home state) vanish.

The enemy truly hates us all equally, and if we are going to survive, we must have impeccable teamwork, trust, and empathy.

The US military is carefully structured around a chain of command for a reason. There is a lot of value in the non-commissioned officer (NCO) ranks and team leaders who make the leadership paradigm so successful and unique. As a team leader, if you do something on your own, you better have a compelling reason.

Getting to that empathetic place also cannot be about false modesty. Everyone must truly contribute to the team based on their individual skillset, fitting together like a puzzle.

If you did not listen to, trust, and respect your team, that was often the difference between life and death.

Big boy rules applied.

LEADERSHIP LESSONS FROM MANUFACTURING

My time in manufacturing was very much about exiting the road of 'my way or the highway' mentality of 1960s-style leadership that often plagues the management ranks.

Textbooks often fail to teach the psychology of successful leaders. I observe many managers trapped within the inside-the-box paradigm. No flex hours, remote or hybrid options. Everyone must punch in at 8:00 a.m. and out at 5:00 p.m. No exceptions—even after a global multiyear pandemic revealed other available options.

Because of GM's unique office politics, I was unable to divulge anything to my union employees. Being a quiet professional and consistent actions allowed me to earn their trust and the belief I had their best interests at heart.

I needed to present a tough-as-nails facade, though I always intended to help my hard-working employees because they directly contributed to my success, along with engineering allies.

Time off request? There was no luxury of blindly saying yes. I knew I would eventually relinquish an approval, nonetheless, they had to pass an interrogation first. (Why do you need the time off, really? You can change the appointment? This a one-time event, correct?)

When one young union employee desperately needed a ride home over an hour away, I chose to stealthily drive him home. Being overly friendly to a union employee could have meant an abrupt career end.

On the flip side, another GM shift manager boasted the best production at the plant and also the highest turnover. He used brash embarrassment, fear, and screaming to control and micromanage his team. His tactics worked...up to a point. He was never promoted to plant manager because no sane supervisor worked on his team. His fear-based leadership created a ceiling on future potential promotions. Additionally, his micromanaging his team was ineffective.

My empathetic approach was not ignored. When my son was close to being born, my workers presented me with lavish baby gifts. When I eventually left GM, the union threw me an amazing, overly generous going-away party complete with thoughtful handmade presents. This was incredibly unusual for someone at the management level. I was genuinely touched that my respectful, human approach to leadership resonated with my workers.

LEADERSHIP LESSONS FROM FINANCE

The transition to finance required a complete shift to the customer service mindset. It also meant mastering 'behavioral finance,' which requires understanding the difference between what finance textbooks teach and what humans actually do.

As a fiduciary financial advisor, I must empathetically understand the burden and responsibility of handling other individual's finances. My recommendations can directly affect their quality of life—now and even generations later.

In my line of work, I have many clients who are business owners. Knowing that, I take the time to understand those individual businesses and how I can guide them to even greater success. To help them capitalize on the unique business and financial opportunities this country offers, they need the finest financial team. Like choosing a security team member in defense contracting or hand-selecting union employees to create the optimal manufacturing team, I arm them with other professionals who can help them plan and prosper. I carefully vet each recommended referral, knowing my character and my firm's reputation are always on the line.

I believe in playing both financial defense and offense. I focus on my client's needs today and their futures. I communicate with them, ensuring they consider important items like creating a will, trust, and planning for long-term care. (I will not work this hard to maximize my client's wealth and watch it evaporated through a third-party medical entity!)

Drawing on my life experiences and education, I treat every client like my own team member. I employ my skills to assist with business benefits, corporate 401(k)'s, estate planning, investment portfolios, college savings, Roth and IRA retirement accounts.

Additionally, I refrain from sugarcoating the truth. If they need to drastically shift strategies, I am diplomatic yet direct.

I also appreciate this trust must be reciprocal. If my client consistently refuses to follow the suggestions or financial plans we devise together,

I will suggest another advisor as a better fit. They must trust me and my expertise, and I also have to trust they will follow through with our strategy.

Together, we are a team.

MANAGING THE FUTURE

I have traded supervising teams for managing financial assets. My job now is primarily advising my clients on their future lives. Successfully doing that with empathy requires me to be their financial quarterback. The advice I give propels them in different, more empowered directions.

I take this role incredibly seriously because it is not just an individual's life that is impacted. Financial literacy, security, and freedom help preserve the future of our democracy.

When America self-funds through successful, thriving small businesses and motivated individuals, politicians lose the ability to merely buy your vote. Your financial freedom preserves your ability to choose politicians based on values and policy—never promises of generous handouts.

Americans need to invest in themselves. When we do, we invest in the very future of our country. I am honored daily to deeply understand my clients and their goals and to play a role in that important process of future financial security.

About Damon

Damon Paull is a Wealth Management Advisor and Marine veteran with a passion for helping individuals and business owners achieve their American Dream. Growing up in Virginia Beach and Kansas City areas, Damon's journey began after an inspiring meeting with legendary Marine sniper, Carlos Hathcock. In the Marines, he was stationed in a California-based infantry unit. Seeking another challenge, he completed the Marine Security Guard school and provided security for prestigious U.S. Embassies, NATO and other U.S. Government facilities in Europe and the Middle East regions.

After his honorable discharge, he utilized his expertise while employed for well-known defense contractors working in sandpits on the Ambassadors Security Detail, the counternarcotics team, and other government agency projects. Following this, he worked for a commodities financial firm specializing in trading oil and gas NYMEX contracts and other Chicago Mercantile Exchange (CME) derivatives.

Damon worked in manufacturing at General Motors before joining AXA – Equitable insurance company. However, it was Damon's life-changing decision to join Totus Wealth Management in Houston, Texas that truly transformed his career. Joining this independent firm enabled him to provide his clients with an extensive range of investment options, adding immense value to their financial portfolios. By empowering clients with diverse investment strategies, Damon and his team create opportunities for them to maximize their financial potential.

Damon's commitment to continuous education and self-improvement is unwavering. He holds an Associate degree in Accounting from American Military University and a Bachelor of Business Administration (BBA) in Finance from the Isenberg School of Management at the University of Massachusetts-Amherst. Additionally, he has successfully completed various industry-recognized certifications, including the Yale School of Management CIMA investments program, Accredited Wealth Management Advisor (AWMA) from the College of Financial Planning, Energy Innovation and Emerging Technologies from Stanford University, and Lean Six Sigma from Villanova University.

Damon is continuously expanding his expertise to better serve his clientele. With an unyielding thirst for knowledge, Damon is currently working towards obtaining the rigorous Certified Investment Management Analyst (CIMA) financial test, completing his Chartered Financial Consultant (ChFC) designation, and finalizing his Master of Science degree in Energy from Texas A&M.

After residing overseas, Damon strongly believes in the free market system. Is there a burning financial issue that keeps you awake at night? After decades of hard work, he believes no one deserves to face financial difficulties.

Damon and his team can be found at the Totus Wealth Management office in sunny Houston, Texas, or visit:

- DamonPaull.com.
- Totus Wealth Management,
  701 North Post Oak Rd. Suite 320,
  Houston, TX 77024

Damon Paull Is a Wealth Managcment Advisor offering securities and advisory services through Cetera Advisors LLC, member FINRA | SIPC, a broker dealer and Registered Investment Advisor. Cetera is under separate ownership from any other named entity.